REPAIRS &
IMPROVEMENTS

REPAIRS &
IMPROVEMENTS
JACKSON & DAY

HarperCollins*Publishers*

Published by HarperCollins Publishers
London

This book was created exclusively for
HarperCollins Publishers by
Jackson Day Jennings Ltd trading as
Inklink.

**Design, art direction
and project management**
Simon Jennings

Text
Albert Jackson
David Day

**Text and
editorial direction**
Albert Jackson

Illustrations editor
David Day

**Designer and
production assistant**
Alan Marshall

Illustrators
David Day
Robin Harris

Additional illustrations
Brian Craker
Michael Parr
Brian Sayers

First published in 1989
This edition published in 1992,
reprinted in 1993

The text and illustrations in this book
were previously published in
Collins Complete DIY Manual

Copyright © 1986, 1989, 1992
HarperCollins Publishers

ISBN 0 00 412815 X

A catalogue record for this book is
available from the British Library

Printed and bound in Hong Kong

Picture credits
Howard Ceilings: 32
Peter Higgins: 41, 54, 59
Magnet & Southerns: 74, 75

CONTENTS

Cross-references
There are few DIY projects that do not require a combination of skills. Decorating a single room, for instance, might also involve modifying the plumbing or electrical wiring, installing ventilation or insulation, repairing the structure of the building and so on. As a result, you might have to refer to more than one section of this book. To help you locate the relevant sections, a symbol (▷) in the text refers you to a list of cross-references in the page margin. Those references printed in bold type are directly related to the task in hand. Other references which will broaden your understanding of the subject are printed in light-weight type.

BRICK HOUSE CONSTRUCTION

Brick-built houses follow a long tradition of styles and methods of construction. The brickwork gives the building character and is the main load-bearing element. If you have to repair and renovate your home it is useful to understand the basic principles of its construction.

Foundations
The foundations carry the whole weight of the house. The type, size and depth are determined largely by the loadbearing properties of the subsoil.

Strip foundation
A continuous strip of concrete set well below ground.

Trench foundation
Similar to the strip type but concrete fills the trench.

Raft foundation
A concrete slab covers the whole ground area.

Support for the house

To support the weight of the structure, most brick-built buildings are supported on a solid base called foundations (See diagrams left).

Wall formation

External walls are loadbearing, supporting roof, floors and internal walls. Cavity walls (◁) comprise two leaves braced with metal ties. Older houses have solid walls (◁) at least 225mm (9in) thick. Bricks are laid with mortar in overlapping bonding patterns to give the wall rigidity. A damp-proof course (DPC) just above ground level prevents moisture rising.

Window and door openings are spanned above with rigid supporting beams called lintels (◁).

Internal walls (◁) are either non-loadbearing divisions made from lightweight blocks, manufactured boards, or timber studding; or loadbearing structures of brick or block.

Solid and timber floors

Ground floors are either solid concrete or suspended timber types (◁). A damp-proof membrane (DPM) is laid between walls where a floor is concrete. With timber floors, sleeper walls of honeycomb brickwork are built on oversite concrete between the base brickwork; a timber sleeper plate rests on each wall and timber joists are supported on them. Their ends may be similarly supported, let into the brickwork or suspended on metal hangers. Floorboards are laid at right angles to joists. First floor joists are supported by the masonry or hangers.

Pitched roof construction

Pitched (sloping) roofs comprise angled rafters fixed to a ridge board, braced by purlins, struts and ties, fixed to wallplates bedded on top of the walls. Roofs are usually clad with slates or tiles to keep the weather out.

TYPICAL COMPONENTS OF A BRICK-BUILT HOUSE

1 Tiles or slates	8 Wall plate	14 Plaster ceiling	20 Ground floor joists
2 Ridge board	9 Lath-and-plaster stud partition	15 Brick loadbearing internal wall	21 Timber sleeper plate
3 Tile battens	10 Internal brick wall	16 Lintel	22 Sleeper wall
4 Roofing felt	11 Brick cavity wall	17 Block partition wall	23 Damp-proof course
5 Purlin	12 Suspended joists	18 Staircase	24 Oversite concrete
6 Rafters	13 Herringbone bracing	19 Floorboards	25 Strip foundation
7 Ceiling joist			26 Ground

TIMBER-FRAMED HOUSE CONSTRUCTION

Timber is an excellent all-purpose material for building and has been used in house construction for centuries. Modern timber-framed houses differ from their brick-built counterparts in that the main structural elements are timber frames, irrespective of whether the walls of the building are clad with brickwork, timber boarding or tiles.

Foundations

As with a brick house, a timber one is built on sound concrete foundations, usually 'strip' or 'raft' types, to spread weight to firm ground.

Wall assembly

Modern timber-framed house walls are constructed with vertical timber studs with horizontal top and bottom plates nailed to them. The frames – which are erected on a concrete slab or a suspended timber platform supported by cavity brick walls – are faced on the outside with plywood sheathing, which stiffens the structure. Breather paper – a moisture barrier – is fixed over the top. Insulation quilt is used between studs.

Stiff timber lintels at openings carry the weight of the upper floor and roof.

Brick cladding is typically used to cover the exterior of the frame, giving the house the appearance of one built from bricks. The cladding is attached to the timber frame with metal ties. Weatherboarding often replaces the brick cladding on upper floors.

Floor construction

Floors in a timber-framed house are either solid concrete or suspended timber, as with a masonry house. In some cases, a concrete floor may be screeded or surfaced with timber or chipboard flooring. Suspended timber floor joists are supported on wallplates and surfaced with chipboard.

Prefabricated roof

Timber-framed houses usually have trussed roofs – prefabricated triangulated frames which combine the rafters and ceiling joists – which are lifted into place and supported by the walls. The trusses are joined together with horizontal and diagonal ties. A ridge board is not fitted, nor are purlins required. Roofing felt, battens and tiling are applied in the usual way.

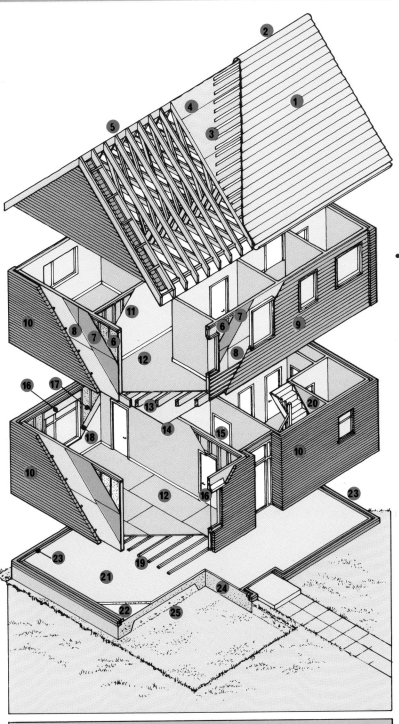

● **Foundation problems**
Consult your Building Control Officer when dealing with problems or new work involving foundations.

Settlement
Settlement cracks in walls are not uncommon, and if not too wide and have stablized they are not a serious problem.

Subsidence
Subsidence caused by weak or shallow foundations or excessive moisture-loss from the ground can be more serious. Widening cracks from window or door openings indicate this.

Heave
Weak foundations can also be damaged by ground swell, or 'heave'.

Light foundations
The walls of extensions or bays with lighter or shallower foundations than the house may show cracks where the two meet due to differential movement.

TYPICAL COMPONENTS OF A TIMBER-FRAMED HOUSE

1 Tiles or slates	8 Breather paper	15 Loadbearing internal	22 Damp-proof
2 Ridge tiles	9 Weatherboarding	stud wall	membrane
3 Tile battens	10 Brick cladding tied	16 Lintel	23 Timber sole plate
4 Roofing felt	to timber frame	17 Insulation	24 Concrete slab
5 Trussed rafters	11 Stud partition	18 Vapour barrier	25 Ground
6 Timber-framed	12 Chipboard floor	19 Floor battens	
loadbearing wall	13 First floor platform	20 Staircase	
7 Plywood sheathing	14 Plasterboard ceiling	21 Concrete screed	

WALLS: EXTERNAL WALLS

Solid walls provide good sound insulation, but poor thermal insulation. There are three basic types: made from brick, block or natural stone. Cavity walls, a relatively modern form of construction, are more effective in preventing moisture penetration and heat loss than solid walls.

SEE ALSO

◁ Details for:
Stretcher bond   78

How solid walls are made

Solid walls are mainly constructed from bonded brickwork or concrete blocks, although local natural stone is also used in certain areas. They're usually at least 225mm (9in) thick – the length of a standard brick – but if they're exposed to severe weather conditions, are frequently a brick and a half thick.

Moisture resistance
Moisture is prevented from penetrating to the inside surface of the wall by evaporation. Rainwater absorbed by the bricks is normally drawn out before it reaches the inner surface. Moisture is prevented from being absorbed from the ground by an impervious damp-proof course (DPC), usually of bituminous felt, set in a bed joint of the brickwork at least 150mm (6in) – two brick courses – from ground level.

Weatherproofing qualities
Many solid walls are cement-rendered or otherwise clad to weatherproof the brickwork. Exterior-grade concrete blocks 225mm (9in) thick can be left exposed but their appearance is improved by rendering. Natural stone walls are usually left bare and weatherproofing relies solely on thickness and density of the material.

Solid walls
Traditional brick and stone walls will vary in thickness according to the age and size of the building. Concrete blocks are now common.

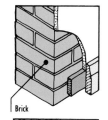
Brick

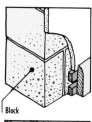
Block

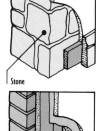
Stone

Cavity walls
This type has replaced solid walls in modern houses. A combination of brick, block and timber frame may be used to construct a cavity wall where brick is usually used for the outer leaf.

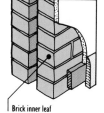
Brick inner leaf

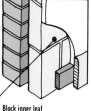
Block inner leaf

Timber inner leaf

How cavity walls are made

Cavity walls consist of two 100mm (4in) thick walls or 'leaves', separated by a 50mm (2in) gap. They may be constructed from bricks, concrete blocks, hollow clay bricks or timber framing, or a combination of these. The stretcher-bonded (◁) leaves must be tied together to make them stable with metal wall ties (See left).

For the cavity to work as a moisture barrier, it is essential that the gap is not bridged. This can happen if mortar collects on the ties during construction.

Where openings occur at a door or window the cavity is closed and a DPC provided to stop moisture seeping in. Weep holes – unmortared vertical joints between every third or fourth brick – are usually provided in the outer leaf above lintels and below the main DPC. Their function is to drain any moisture from the cavity that penetrates the outer leaf.

Cavity walls may be given improved thermal insulation by installing insulating panels as the wall is built, or filling with an insulating material later on.

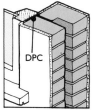
Vertical DPC at window opening in cavity wall.

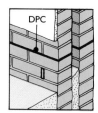
Weep holes are formed below main DPC.

Cavity ties
Cavity wall ties are laid in the bed joints at 900mm (3ft) spacings horizontally and 450mm (1ft 6in) vertically and staggered on alternate rows.

Wire butterfly tie

Sheet metal tie

IDENTIFYING LOADBEARING AND NON-LOADBEARING WALLS

The external walls of the house transmit the loads of suspended timber floors, most of the roof and other structures to the foundations. Usually all the external walls are loadbearing. The floor and ceiling joists and other internal walls might also be carried on loadbearing internal walls.

Not all internal walls are loadbearing or 'structural', however: loadbearing walls can be identified by their position in the structure, and the materials used in their construction.

A wall which carries the floor joists will have the floorboards running parallel with it. Check at each floor level as a wall which passes through the centre of the house may carry the first floor but not the ground floor. Floor joists are usually run in the direction of the shortest span. Check roof braces, which may bear on an internal wall.

Loadbearing walls are usually made of brick or loadbearing concrete blocks. Occasionally, wooden stud walls are used to carry some weight. A wall may also be termed loadbearing or structural where it is not carrying a load but is adding to the stability of the structure, perhaps stiffening an adjacent wall.

Non-loadbearing walls
Walls which divide the floor space into rooms, and not intended to support the structure, are known as non-loadbearing. They may be made of brick, lightweight concrete blocks, timber studding or cellular core wallboard, and are usually only a single storey in height. If the floorboards run under the wall you can safely assume that the wall is non-loadbearing.

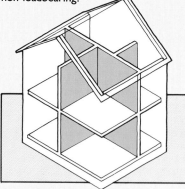
Non-loadbearing walls
These walls divide the internal space into smaller rooms and are relatively lightweight.

INTERNAL WALLS

There are basically two types of internal wall: party walls, which divide houses built side by side, and partition walls, which divide up the space within the house. The former are structural, the latter load or non-loadbearing.

Party wall construction

Party walls, or separating walls, are shared solid walls which divide houses built side by side. Party walls separate the properties over the entire height of the building to prevent the spread of fire and provide good sound insulation.

Partition walls

Internal partition walls can be loadbearing or non-loadbearing, but are usually relatively lightweight and not more than one brick thick. Partition walls for houses may be made from brick, concrete blocks, hollow clay blocks, timber framing or cellular core wallboard (See below). A plaster finish is usually applied to brick or block walls for a smooth surface.

Stud-partition walls
Timber-framed partitions called stud walls are common in new and old houses. They are usually made from 100m (4in) wide sawn softwood. The vertical timbers, called studs, may be placed 350mm (1ft 2in), 400mm (1ft 4in) or 600mm (2ft) apart. Diagonal braces may be included for strength.

Laths – thin strips of wood nailed horizontally to the studs – are used as a key for plaster in old houses; plasterboard has now replaced lath-and-plaster on this type of wall. Although stud walls are usually non-loadbearing, they can carry a lateral load.

Stud walls offer a convenient duct for running services such as wiring but because of their hollow construction, special fixings are required when attaching anything to the surface ($\triangleright$).

Lightweight concrete blocks
Blocks are widely used for modern partition walls. They're made to course with bricks and are nominally 150 to 225mm (6 to 9in) high and 450 or 600mm (1ft 6in or 2ft) long.

The most common size is 450 x 225mm (1ft 6in x 9in) and a range of thicknesses from 50 to 300mm (2 to 12in) is available – use the 100mm (4in) wide block for a partition wall. This size corresponds to standard brick bonding, being equal to three courses high and two bricks long. Blocks are grey in colour, made from cement and lightweight aggregate. Their large size makes building a wall quick and simple. They provide good sound and thermal insulation and are fireproof. Fixings can be made at any point on the wall using special plugs, and services can be channelled into the surface. Blocks are cut easily with a bolster chisel.

Hollow clay blocks
Clay blocks are red in colour, may be smooth-faced or horizontally grooved as a key for a plaster coating, and are hollow for a lightweight wall that has good sound and thermal insulation properties and is fireproof. Hollow clay blocks do not take nails well; fixings should be made with screws and suitable cavity fixings. Where nailing is required – for fixing skirtings or door linings, for example – solid blocks would be incorporated.

Cellular-core wallboard
This manufactured wall panel is made from two sheets of plasterboard with a gridded cardboard core bonded between them. It is available in similar sizes to standard plasterboard sheets, and 50, 56 or 63mm (2, 2¼ or 2½in) thick. The cell structure makes a light but rigid partitioning that is simple to install and can be decorated directly or finished with plaster. All fixings to this type of wall require a screwed cavity device unless wooden plugs are fitted during erection. The plugs are short lengths of the battening used to fix the panels together. It is necessary to pre-plan the placing of the fixtures before the plugs are driven into the core from the edge. The face of the board is marked to indicate the positions of the plugs before the partition is assembled. Clear channels for cable or pipe runs before assembly.

SEE ALSO

Details for: $\triangleright$
Cavity fixings | 25
Cellular-core partitions | 26–27
Traditional plastering | 34
Plasterboard | 40

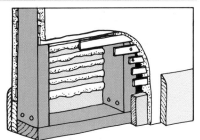
Lath-and-plaster stud partition

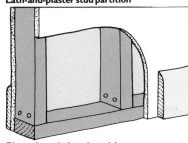
Plasterboarded stud partition

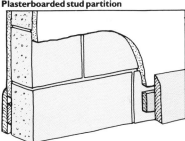
Plastered concrete block partition

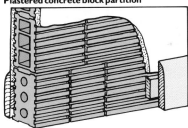
Plastered hollow clay-block partition

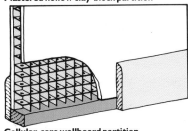
Cellular-core wallboard partition

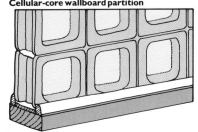
Glass-block partition

Glass blocks
Hollow glass blocks can be used for non-loadbearing feature walls. Made in square and rectangular shapes and a range of colours they can be laid in mortar or dry-fixed with plastic jointing strips in a frame.

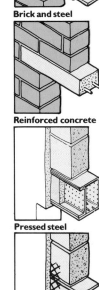

Stone and timber

Brick and steel

Reinforced concrete

Pressed steel

Rolled steel

TYPES OF LINTEL

A lintel bridges the gap above an opening. The type used will depend on the size of the opening and availability.

WOOD

Wooden lintels were commonly built into the brick walls of older houses, often in exterior walls, behind a stone lintel or brick arch. They can suffer from rot due to penetrating damp, but are still used in timber-framed houses.

BRICK

Brick lintels are used with wood, steel or concrete lintels over external openings but are not strong. Some are supported by a flat or angled metal bar.

STONE

A feature of the exterior of older houses, stone is not strong in tension and cannot be used for wide spans. The stone block does not usually support the full thickness of the wall – a timber lintel is often used behind it.

CONCRETE

Concrete lintels are used for interior and exterior openings. Concrete is good in compression but not in tension. To overcome this, metal rods are embedded in the lower portion of the beam to reinforce it. Prestressed concrete lintels, reinforced with wire strands set in the concrete under tension, are lighter than other concrete lintels. Concrete lintels are made in a range of sizes to match brick and block courses and to suit various wall thickness. Though capable of spanning large openings, their weight can make handling awkward.

STEEL

Galvanized pressed steel lintels are widely used for internal and external openings. They are designed for cavity and solid walls of brick and block or timber-framed construction. Versions for cavity walls include a tray to channel moisture to the outside. Standard sections and lengths are available and are fairly lightweight. Some are perforated for plastering direct.

Heavyweight rolled steel joists (RSJs) are mainly used when making two rooms into one (◁). The supplier will cut the I-section beam to length.

SPANNING OPENINGS IN WALLS

A doorway, window or hatchway requires an opening to be created in the wall. In a loadbearing wall, the top of the opening must be built to carry the structure above – even cutting a hole in a partition means propping the masonry.

Where supports are needed

Door or window frames aren't designed to carry superimposed loads, so the load from floors above – even the brickwork above the opening – must be supported by a rigid beam called a lintel, which transmits the weight to the sides where the bearings are firm. Wider openings call for stronger beams, such as rolled steel joists (RSJs). There are numerous beams, but all work in the same way.

The forces on a beam

When a load is placed at the centre of a beam supported at each end, the beam will bend. The lower portion is being stretched and is in 'tension'; the top portion is being squeezed and is in 'compression'. The beam is also subjected to 'shear' forces where the vertical load is trying to sever the beam at the points of support. A beam must be able to resist these forces. This is achieved by the correct choice of material and the depth of the beam in relation to the imposed load and the span of the opening.

Calculating lintel size

The purpose of a lintel is to form a straight bridge across an opening, which can carry the load of the structure above it. The load may be relatively light, being no more than a number of brick or block courses. It is more likely that other loads from upper floors and the roof will also bear on the lintel.

The size of the lintel must be suitable for the job it has to do. The size should be derived from calculations based on the weight of the materials used in the construction of the building. Calculation for specifying a beam is a job for an architect or structural engineer. Tables relating to the weight of the materials are used on which to base the figures.

In practice, for typical situations, a builder can help you decide on the required size of lintel based on his experience. A Building Control Officer will be happy to accept this type of specification but he can insist that proper calculations are submitted with your application for Building Regulations approval.

When to support a wall

If you are creating a door, window or hatchway which is no wider than 1m (3ft) across in a non-loadbearing wall you can cut the hole without having to support the walling above providing the wall is properly bonded and sound. The only area of brickwork that is likely to collapse is roughly in the shape of a 45 degree triangle directly above the opening leaving a self-supporting stepped arch of brickwork. This effect is known as self-corbelling. Do not rely on the self-corbelling effect to support the wall if you plan to make an opening which is more than 1m (3ft) wide. In that case, temporarily support the wall as if it were loadbearing.

Before you make any opening in a loadbearing wall you will need to erect adjustable props (◁) as temporary supports, not only for the weight of the masonry but also for the loads that bear on it from floors, walls and roof above.

Self-corbelling
The shaded bricks are the only ones at risk of falling out before the lintel is installed because of the self-corbelling effect of the bricks above. Theoretically the lintel supports the weight of the materials within the 60 degree triangle plus any superimposed floor or roof loading, but when the side walls (piers) are narrow, the load on the lintel is increased to encompass the area of the rectangle.

RIGGING UP ADJUSTABLE PROPS

To remove part of a loadbearing wall it's necessary to temporarily support the wall above the opening. Hire adjustable steel props (▷) and scaffold boards to spread the load across the floor. Where the brickwork will remain below the ceiling level, you will also need 'needles' to spread the load. Needles must be of sawn timber at least 150 x 100mm (6 x 4in) in section and about 1.8m (6ft) long.

For a hatchway or door opening, probably only one needle and two props will suffice: place the needle centrally over the opening about 150mm (6in) above the lintel position. For wider openings, or where a load is great, two needles and four props will be needed, spaced no more than 1m (3ft) apart across the width of the opening.

Chop a hole in the wall for each needle and slot them through. Support each end with a prop, which works like a car jack. Stand the props on scaffold boards no more than 600mm (2ft) from each side of the wall.

Solid wall
Locate joints before cutting the slot.

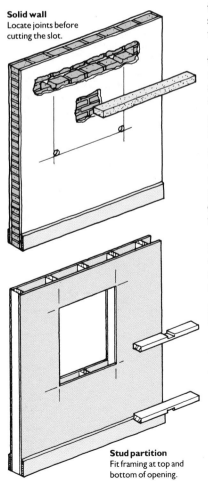

Stud partition
Fit framing at top and bottom of opening.

MAKING A HATCHWAY

A serving hatch is a convenient opening in a wall, usually between a kitchen and dining area, through which you can pass food, drinks and equipment. If you are blocking off a doorway, or making a stud wall, it may be advantageous to allow for a hatch. You may want to make a hatchway in an existing wall.

Planning the size and shape

Ideally the bottom of the opening should be an extension of the kitchen worktop or at least flush with a work surface: 900mm (3ft) is a comfortable working height and the standard height for kitchen worktops. For practicality – passing through a tray and serving dishes, for instance – it should not be narrower than 750mm (2ft 6in).

Hatches should be fitted with some means of closing the opening for privacy, preventing cooking smells from drifting and, in some cases, as a fire-check (See right).

Creating the opening

You can make a hatchway in either a loadbearing or a solid non-loadbearing wall in much the same way: the main requirement with the former is temporarily supporting the masonry above and the load imposed on the wall. Mark the position for the hatch on one side of the wall. Align the hole with the vertical and horizontal mortar courses between bricks or blocks to save having to cut too many bricks – hack off a square of plaster at the centre to locate the joints.

Mark out the shape and position of the opening on the other side of the wall using adjacent walls, the ceiling and floor as references, or drill through at the corners. Make the hole about 25mm (1in) oversize to allow for fitting a lining frame. Mark the lintel position.

Set up adjustable props and needles if you're working on a loadbearing wall (See left), then chop a slot for the lintel with a club hammer and bolster chisel – on a brick wall this will probably be a single course of bricks deep; on a block wall, remove a whole course of blocks and fill the gap with bricks. Trowel mortar onto the bearings and lift on the lintel. Use a spirit level to check that the lintel is perfectly horizontal – pack under it with pieces of slate if necessary. Replace any bricks above the lintel that have dropped. Leave for 24 hours to set, then remove props and needles and hack away the masonry below.

Making a hatchway in a stud wall

Cutting an opening in a stud partition wall is simpler than making one in a solid wall, but if the wall bears some weight you'll need to support the floor or ceiling above with props using planks to spread the load.

Mark out, then cut away the plasterboard or lath-and-plaster covering from each side to expose the studs. For a hatch the width between studs (about 450mm/1ft 6in), just skew-nail a nogging between them at the top and bottom of the opening. If it's to be wider, make the opening span three studs. Cut away part of the middle stud at the height you want the hatch, allowing for the thickness of a horizontal frame member above and below the opening. Make the framing from studding timber and cut them to fit between the two studs on each side of the cut one. Fit and check for level.

Fitting a lining frame

Line the four sides of the hatch opening with 25mm (1in) thick planed softwood joined at the corners with butt joints or bare-faced tongued and grooved joints (▷) for a neater result. The frame can either finish flush with the plaster wall surface and be covered with an architrave, or it can project beyond the plaster to form a lip or shelf.

The sides of the opening in a masonry wall are likely to be rough – it's not easy to chop a clean line. Make and fit the frame, then pack out the gap between masonry and lining with offcuts of wood – the frame must be truly square within the opening; check this with a spirit level. Screw the frame to the masonry using fixing plugs, fitted when the frame is positioned. Make good with mortar all round it. Rake back the surface of the mortar and when set finish flush with plaster.

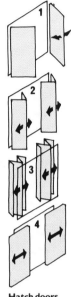

Hatch doors
1 Double-hinged
2 Twin bi-fold
3 Concertina
4 Horizontal-sliding

Finishing the frame
Use an architrave to cover the joint between the lining and wall or let the frame project to mask it.

Fit an architrave

Let frame project

11

CUTTING AN INTERNAL DOORWAY

1 Fix galvanized ties

2 Nail to wedges

Making a doorway in an existing wall may be necessary if you're changing the use of the room or improving its layout: this is typical when converting a kitchen, where fitted units dictate the positions of access and exit doors. As with fitting a hatchway (◁), it's necessary to install a lintel to ensure the stability of the wall itself and any other load which bears on it.

Preparing a brick or block wall

First check whether the wall is non-loadbearing or loadbearing (◁). If the former, seek approval from the Building Control Officer (BCO). Mark the opening on one side of the wall, then examine the coursing of the bricks or blocks by exposing a small area; move the opening if necessary to align the perimeter with the vertical joints.

The height should allow for the height of the door plus 10mm (⅜in) tolerance, the thickness of the soffit lining and a new concrete or steel lintel. The width of the opening should be the width of the door plus 6mm (¼in) tolerance and twice the thickness of the door jamb lining. Allow a further 12mm (½in) for fitting the lining.

Carefully prise off the skirtings from both sides of the wall. They can be cut and reused later. Prop the wall and fit the lintel (See right) before cutting out the bulk of the masonry. Leave overnight for the bearings to set hard. The next day, starting from the top just below the lintel, chop out the individual bricks using a club hammer and bolster chisel. At the sides of the opening cut the half or three-quarter bricks protruding into the doorway. Chop downwards where you can. If the wall is built from lightweight blocks, use a universal hand saw or a masonry saw (◁) to slice through the bonding.

Bag up the rubble frequently in stout polythene sacks and stack whole bricks out of the way for re-use. Spray the area with water from a plant sprayer to settle the dust.

At the bottom, chop out the brickwork to just below floor level so that you can continue the flooring(◁).

Fitting the door lining

You'll have to fit a timber frame within the new doorway to which you can attach the stop-bead, door and decorative architrave (◁). Make the frame from planed timber 25mm (1in) thick and the width of the wall. Fit the lining (◁) to the sides of the opening with galvanized metal frame cramps (**1**) mortared into slots cut in the brickwork, or fit wooden wedges in the mortar joints and nail the frame to them (See diagram (**2**) left).

Dealing with a stud wall

First locate the positions of the studs (◁), then prise off the skirting. Mark out the position for the opening on the wall then remove the plasterwork. For lath-and-plaster walls, chop through to the laths with a bolster chisel, then saw the strips off. For a plasterboard wall, saw through the cladding or use a sharp trimming knife. If there are studs on each side of the opening, cut the laths or plasterboard flush with these timbers. The hole position often won't correspond with the studs, so cut back to the centre of the nearest stud on each side. Cut one or two studs to the required height—door plus 10mm (⅜in) tolerance and the lining thickness plus a 50mm (2in) head member.

Level up and skew-nail the head member to the remaining studs at each end. Also dovetail-nail it to the ends of the cut studs. Saw through and remove the floor plate to the width of the door, plus 6mm (¼in) tolerance and twice the thickness of the door lining. Cut and nail the new studs, which will form the door jambs, to fit between the head and sill. Fit noggings between the new and original stud or studs. Cut and nail plasterboard to fill the gaps between the original wall surface and the new studs. Make and fit the door lining (◁). Finish the surfaces with plaster (◁), fit the architraves and replace the skirting.

Alternatively, cut the cladding from floor to ceiling and refit the studding flush with the cut edge. Mark the width of the opening, saw through the plaster from both sides of the wall then strip the plasterwork and knock out the exposed studs and noggings. Cut the floor sill level with the plaster and remove. Drive the studs into the cut edges until flush. Nail them at top and bottom. Fit a door head member between them and a short vertical stud above it. Cover the space above the doorway with plasterboard.

INSTALLING THE LINTEL

Draw in the position for the lintel, allowing a margin for fitting tolerance. Chop a groove around the perimeter of the opening with a club hammer and bolster chisel, then hack off the plaster. Fit adjustable metal props and needles (◁), then cut a slot for the lintel. Bed a concrete lintel in a mortar mix of 1 part cement: 3 parts sand on bearings no narrower than 150mm (6in) at each side of the slot, and set level. Pack underneath with pieces of slate to wedge it horizontal. Replace loose bricks and fill any gaps with the same mortar mix.

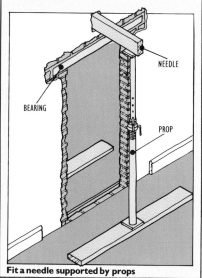

NEEDLE

BEARING

PROP

Fit a needle supported by props

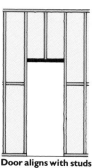

Door aligns with studs

Door is misaligned

Making the frame
The method you adopt for the frame will depend on the positions of the studs. The diagrams illustrate typical solutions.

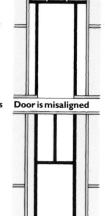

Studs repositioned

FILLING AN OPENING IN A STUD PARTITION

Strip the door lining as described (See right). Trim the lath-and-plaster or plasterboard back to the centre line of the door jamb studs and head member, with a sharp trimming knife. Lever out the old nails with a claw hammer. Nail the new cut edge all round.

Nail a matching sill to the floor between the studs. Cut and nail a new stud centrally between head and sill. Cut and nail noggings between the studs across the opening. Fix plasterboard to each face of the opening. Cut the board 3mm (⅛in) less all round. Fill and tape the joints (▷), then finish as required with wallcovering or tiles.

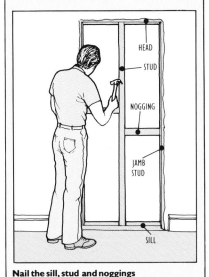

Nail the sill, stud and noggings

HEAD
STUD
NOGGING
JAMB STUD
SILL

BLOCKING OFF A DOORWAY

If you are making a new opening in a wall, it's possible that you will also have to block off the original one.

Obviously, you'll want the patch to be invisible, which takes careful plastering or joint filling of plasterboard.

Choosing the right materials

It is generally better to fill in the opening with the same materials used in the construction of the wall – although you can consider bricks and blocks as the same – to prevent cracks forming due to movement in the structure. You could use a wooden stud frame with a plasterboard lining and plaster finish to fill an opening in a brick wall, but it would not have the same acoustic properties as a solid infill and cracks are difficult to prevent or disguise.

Removing the woodwork

Saw through the door jamb linings close to the top and prise them away from the brickwork with a wrecking bar. Start levering at the bottom. If the linings were fitted before the flooring, the ends could be trapped: cut them flush with the floor. Next, prise the soffit board away from the top.

Bricking up the opening

Cut back the plaster about 150mm (6in) all round the opening. It need not be an even line; unevenness helps to disguise the outline of the doorway.

To bond the new brickwork into the old, cut out a half-brick on each side of the opening at every fourth course, using a club hammer and bolster chisel. For a block wall, remove a quarter of a block from alternate courses.

It's not vital to tooth-in the infill if you're using blocks (which are easy and quick to lay) as it will require more cutting to fit. Instead, 100mm (4in) cut clasp nails driven dovetail fashion into the bed joints of the side brickwork **(1)** can be used to tie the masonry together. Galvanized metal frame cramps can also be used to save cutting into the bricks **(2)** – screw them to the wall, resting on every fourth brick.

Lay the bricks or blocks in mortar, following the original courses. If a wooden suspended floor runs through the opening, lay the bricks on a timber sole plate nailed across the opening. When the mortar has set, spread on a base coat of plaster, followed by a finishing coat (▷). Fit two complete lengths of new matching skirting, or add to the original. When making up the skirting from old pieces, make sure the joints do not occur in the same place as the original opening.

SEE ALSO

Details for: ▷	
Plasterwork	34–39
Taping joints	46
Fitting skirting	59
Door casings	61

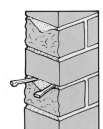

1 Nail ties

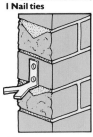

2 Frame cramp

Cut out half-bricks

Lay bricks into the courses

Cut blocks to match bonding

13

CONVERTING TWO ROOMS TO ONE

Making a through room is the best way to improve access between areas frequently used – the dining and living rooms, for instance – and of course expands your living space considerably. The job uses similar principles to making a hatchway or a new doorway, although on a much larger scale. Removing a dividing wall – whether it's structural or simply a non-loadbearing partition – is a major undertaking, but it needn't be daunting. If you follow some basic safety and rigid structural rules, much of the job is straightforward, if messy and disruptive. Before you start, plan out your requirements and consult the at-a-glance flow chart, right, for a break-down of just what's involved.

WHY DO YOU WANT A THROUGH ROOM?

Before you go ahead and demolish the wall between two rooms, consider just how the new space might function, its appearance, the time it will take you to carry out the work, and the cost.

Ask yourself the following questions:
- Will the shape and size of the new room suit your needs? Remember, if you have a young family, your needs are likely to change as they grow up.
- Will most of the family activities be carried out in the same room (eating, watching TV, playing music, reading, conversation, playing with toys, hobbies, homework)?
- Will removing the wall deprive you of privacy within the family, or from passers-by in the street?
- Will the new room feel like one unit and not a conversion? For example, do the skirtings and mouldings match? Are the fireplaces acceptable when seen together, or should one be removed? Should one of the doorways, if close together, be blocked off?
- Will the loss of a wall make the furniture arrangements difficult – particularly if central heating radiators are in use and take up valuable wall space elsewhere?
- Will the heating and lighting need to be modified?
- Will the proposed shape of the opening be in character with the room and the right proportion?

● **Hiring professionals**
If you're in doubt, hire a professional builder: to save costs, you may be able to work as a labourer or do preparation and clearing work .

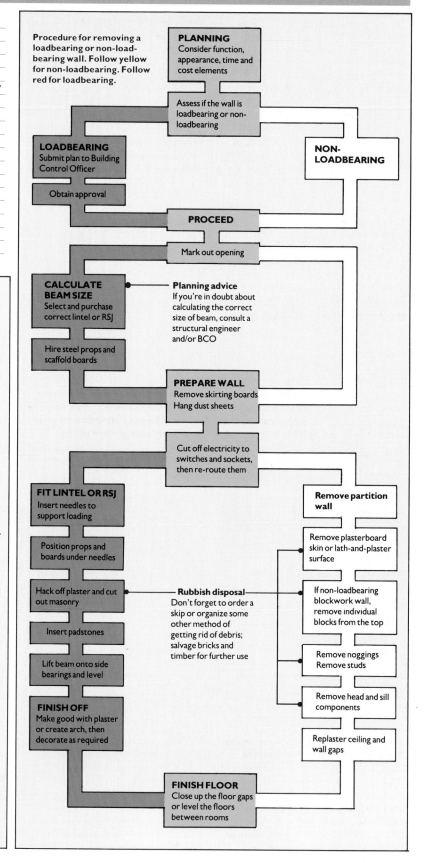

Procedure for removing a loadbearing or non-load-bearing wall. Follow yellow for non-loadbearing. Follow red for loadbearing.

PLANNING
Consider function, appearance, time and cost elements

Assess if the wall is loadbearing or non-loadbearing

LOADBEARING
Submit plan to Building Control Officer

Obtain approval

NON-LOADBEARING

PROCEED

Mark out opening

CALCULATE BEAM SIZE
Select and purchase correct lintel or RSJ

Hire steel props and scaffold boards

Planning advice
If you're in doubt about calculating the correct size of beam, consult a structural engineer and/or BCO

PREPARE WALL
Remove skirting boards
Hang dust sheets

Cut off electricity to switches and sockets, then re-route them

FIT LINTEL OR RSJ
Insert needles to support loading

Position props and boards under needles

Hack off plaster and cut out masonry

Insert padstones

Lift beam onto side bearings and level

FINISH OFF
Make good with plaster or create arch, then decorate as required

Rubbish disposal
Don't forget to order a skip or organize some other method of getting rid of debris; salvage bricks and timber for further use

Remove partition wall

Remove plasterboard skin or lath-and-plaster surface

If non-loadbearing blockwork wall, remove individual blocks from the top

Remove noggings
Remove studs

Remove head and sill components

Replaster ceiling and wall gaps

FINISH FLOOR
Close up the floor gaps or level the floors between rooms

SUPPORTING THE STRUCTURAL WALL

Once you have satisfied yourself that the opening will be an improvement to your home's layout, consider the practical problems: first determine whether or not the wall is loadbearing or a non-loadbearing partition ($\triangleright$).

Mark out the proposed opening on the wall with chalk to help you visualise its size and proportion. Bear in mind that a loadbearing wall will need a beam spanning the opening with at least 150mm (6in) bearings at each end.

Choosing a beam

The most suitable beam for a through room is usually a rolled steel joist (RSJ), although this type of beam will require special preparation before it can be plastered over. Reinforced and pre-stressed concrete lintels can also be used for openings up to about 3m (10ft), but, over a wide span, their considerable weight makes them difficult to handle; pre-stressed types are lighter but best suited to single door or hatch openings ($\triangleright$) rather than wide spans. Pressed steel box lintels – available in lengths up to 5.4m (about 18ft) – are much lighter and can be plastered directly.

What size beam?
For specifying an RSJ the following rule of thumb can be employed, although exact details depend on the particular location and the result must be approved by the Building Control Officer. For pressed steel lintels, refer to the manufacturer for sizes:

CALCULATING THE SIZE OF A BEAM
A rule-of-thumb guide used by builders
Make beam 25mm (1in) deep for every 300mm (1ft) span.

Height of opening

The height of the opening is to some extent determined by the height of the ceiling and the depth of the beam. The depth of the beam is determined by the width of the opening it has to span, and the load it must carry. Consult an architect or structural engineer who, for a fee, can calculate this for you. The beam can be positioned directly under the ceiling joists of a low ceiling.

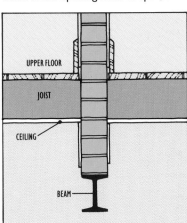

Brickwork supported below ceiling level

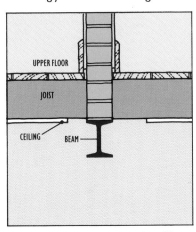

Brickwork supported directly under ceiling

Applying for permission

Before any work is started on a loadbearing wall you must seek approval from your local authority's Building Control Officer. He will require a drawing showing the proposed opening, its overall height and width and how the structure above the opening is to be supported. This need not be drawn up by a professional, but it should be clear. Approval is unlikely to be withheld providing the work complies with the Building Regulations. The BCO must be satisfied that the removal of the wall will not weaken the structure of the house, or any buildings attached to it, and that it does not encourage the spread of fire. Where a party wall is involved, it will be necessary to get written approval from your neighbour. The BCO will advise you.

HOW A BEAM IS SUPPORTED

The supports are usually brick piers, which are in effect columns attached to the side walls and formed from the remainder of the old wall. Concrete padstones are required on which to sit the beam. The BCO may want the piers increased in thickness to give sufficient support to the beam and the side flanking wall.

Ideally, it would be better if no piers were used as they interrupt the line of the side walls running through. It might be possible to run the ends of the beam into the walls, eliminating the need for piers, but this must be subject to local approval. It would require a horizontal concrete beam called a spreader set in the wall to distribute the load across more of the wall.

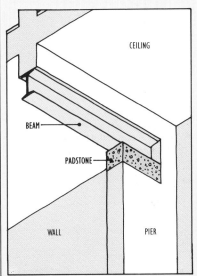

Pier capped by padstone supports the beam

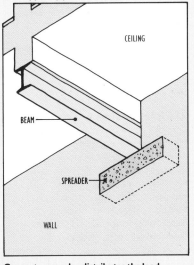

Concrete spreader distributes the load

15

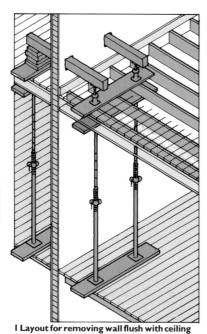

1 Layout for removing wall flush with ceiling

Supporting the wall

1 When removing a wall up to ceiling level, support the upper floor with scaffold boards and props alone when the joists pass through the brickwork to support the wall. Otherwise, in addition, use needles on jacks placed directly above the props.
2 Normally brickwork projects below the ceiling level and is supported on needles passing through holes in the wall.

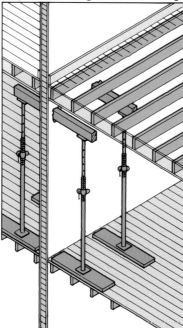

2 Layout for removing wall below ceiling

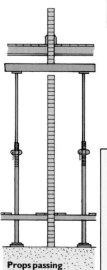

Props passing through the suspended floor

TRANSFER THE LOAD TO THE SUBFLOOR

If the floor appears to spring when you jump on it, consult a builder to make sure the floor can carry the weight imposed. It may be necessary to lift some of the floorboards and support the props on the foundations. In older houses, where there is no concrete below the floor, scaffold boards must be placed under the props to spread the load over the ground.

REMOVING THE WALL

To remove part of a loadbearing wall you must temporarily support the walling above the opening. You will need to hire adjustable steel props (◁), and scaffold boards on which to support them. Where the beam is to be placed at ceiling level, hire extra boards to support the ceiling **(1)**. Generally you will have to fit needles through the wall to transfer the load to the props **(2)**. The needles must be at least 150 × 100mm (6 × 4in) in section.

Hire sufficient props to be spaced not more than 1m (3ft) apart across the width of the opening. If possible, buy the beam after the Building Control Officer's inspection. It can then be cut to your exact requirements.

Preparation and marking out

Remove the skirting boards from both sides of the wall (◁). Working from one side, mark out the position of the beam on the wall in pencil. Use a steel tape measure, spirit level and straightedge for accuracy.

Hang dust sheets around the work area on the opposite face of the wall to help contain much of the inevitable airborne dust; attach them with battens nailed over them at the top. Seal gaps around all doors with masking tape to prevent the dust from travelling throughout the house. Open windows in the rooms you're working in.

Inserting the needles

Mark the positions for the needles on the wall, then cut away the plaster locally and chisel a hole through the brickwork at each point. Finish level with the bottom of one course of bricks. Make the holes slightly oversize So you can easily pass the needles through. Position a pair of adjustable props under each needle not more than 600mm (2ft) from each side of the wall. Stand the props on scaffold boards to spread the load over the floor.

Adjust the props to take the weight of the structure and nail their base plates to the supporting boards to prevent them being dislodged.

Supporting the ceiling

If the ceiling needs supporting, stand the props on scaffold boards at each side of the wall and adjust so they're virtually to ceiling height – they should be placed 600mm (2ft) from the wall. Place another plank on top of the pairs of props and adjust simultaneously until the ceiling joists are supported.

Removing the wall

Hack off the plaster using a club hammer and bolster chisel, then start to cut out the brickwork, working from the top. Once you've removed four or five courses, cut the bricks at the side of the opening. Chop downwards with the bolster pointing in towards the wall to cut the bricks cleanly. Remove all the brickwork down to one course below the floorboards. Clear the rubble as you work into stout polythene sacks – it may be worth hiring a skip. The job is slow and extremely laborious, but you can make it easier and quicker using a power brick-cutting saw (See below).

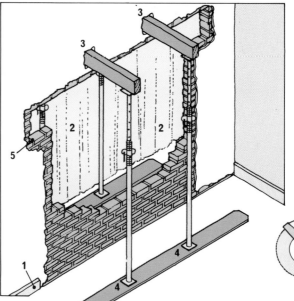

Cutting the opening
1 Remove or cut back the skirting and mark the beam's position.
2 Hang dust sheets around the work area.
3 Cut openings and insert needles.
4 Stand props on scaffold boards and adjust them to support the needles.
5 Cut away the plaster, then chisel out the bricks starting from the top of the opening.

Brick-cutting saw

PLACING THE BEAM

Building piers

If the wall you're removing is deemed unsuitable as a basis for the supporting piers, you have two other choices. Where the adjacent wall is double thickness, you may be able to cut a hole to take the end of the beam allowing the weight to be distributed to the existing foundations. If this isn't possible, you'll have to build new piers with their own foundations. The piers must be built below the floor on concrete padstones cast on hardcore; they must include a DPC – engineering bricks may suffice – and must themselves be bonded in single – or double – brick thickness and toothed at every fourth course into the brickwork of the adjoining wall. The BCO will tell you the size for the piers.

Installing the beam

Make two wooden forms or boxes from thick plywood or softwood and cast concrete padstones (on which to bed the RSJ) to the size required by the BCO. Mix the concrete to the proportions 1 part cement: 2 parts sand: 4 parts aggregate. When set, bed the padstones in mortar at the top of each pier. When a large padstone is required, it may be better to cast it in situ: set up formwork at the required height on each side and check the level between the two.

Build a work platform by placing doubled-up scaffold boards between steady stepladders, or hire scaffold tower sections. You'll need help to lift the beam into position.

Apply mortar to the padstones, then lift and set the RSJ in place. Pack pieces of slate between the beam and the brickwork above to fill out the gap. Alternatively, 'dry-pack' the gap with a mortar mix of 1 part cement: 3 parts sand, which is just wet enough to bind it together. Work it well into the gap with a bricklaying trowel and compact it with a wooden batten and a hammer. Where the gap can take a whole brick or more, apply a bed of mortar and rebuild the brickwork on top of the beam. Work the course between the needles so that when the timbers are removed the holes can be filled in to continue the bonding. Allow two days for the mortar to set, then remove the props and the needles and fill in the holes.

When the beam is fitted against ceiling joists you can use a different method. Support the ceiling with props and a board to spread the load (See left), on each side of the wall. Cut away the wall, then lift the beam into position and fit a pair of adjustable props under it. Apply mortar to the top of the beam and screw up the props to push it against the joists and brickwork above. Bed padstones in mortar or build formwork at each end and cast them.

FINISHING THE BEAM

A steel beam should be enclosed to provide protection from fire (which would cause it to distort) and to give a flat surface that can be decorated. Wet plaster, plasterboard or a specially made fireproof board can be used.

Cladding with plaster
Box in an RSJ with expanded galvanized metal mesh to provide a key for the plaster. Fold the mesh around the beam, then lap it up onto the brickwork above and secure with galvanized nails.

Alternatively, wedge shaped wooden blocks (soldiers) into the recessed sides of the beam and nail the expanded metal to these. It's a good idea to prime the cut edges of the mesh to prevent corrosion which can stain the plaster.

Making good with plasterboard
To box in the beam with plasterboard, you will need to fit shaped wooden blocks, wedged into the sides. To these fix wooden battens nailed together to make fixings for the plasterboard panels (if you plan to install a folding door system in the opening, you can nail the door lining directly to these same fixings (▷). Set the plasterboard about 3mm (⅛in) below plaster level to allow for a skim coat to finish flush with the surrounding wall. Fill and seal the joints with tape (▷).

Plaster the piers, then finish the beam and pier together.

Disguising the beam
You can conceal the angular RSJ by fitting a simulated oak beam, moulded from rigid urethane foam plastic, which can be simply glued or nailed over the beam, to give a country cottage effect to the room.

SEE ALSO	
Details for: ▷	
Plasterboard	46–47
Door casings	61, 64
Supporting a beam	15
Plasterwork	34–39

● **Finishing a pressed-steel beam**
Pressed-steel box-profile beams are made with perforated faces to provide a key for the plaster.

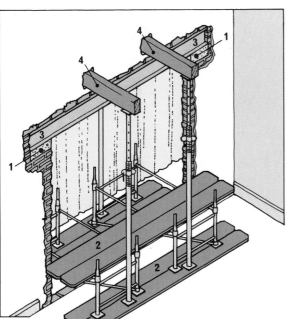

Installing the beam
1 Cast concrete padstones and set them on the brickwork piers.
2 Set up a secure platform to enable two people to work safely.
3 Place the beam on the mortared padstones and check level. Fill the gaps between the beam and the brickwork.
4 When set remove the props and needles and fill the holes.

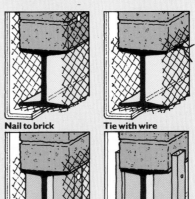

Nail to brick   Tie with wire

Or nail to blocks   Or use plasterboard

FITTING ARCHES

Removing a dividing wall – to create a through living-and-dining room, for instance – leaves you with a boxy break formed by the RSJ and its piers. The angularity might suit your decor and furnishings, but for a softer look, an arch is the answer: you can buy ready-made arch formers, which you fix in the opening and plaster over; for an individual profile, however, it's quite straightforward to make your own arch using wet plaster or plasterboard.

Deciding on the arch profile

It's advisable to plan for the installation of an arch before you make your opening. Choose the style of arch carefully: the shape will effectively lower the height of the opening at the sides, which may be impracticable and poorly proportioned for the room.

Corner arches simply round off the angle and don't encroach on headroom; semi-circular types give a full, rounded shape but eat into headroom at the sides; pointed arches make a distinctive shape without taking up headroom at the middle of the opening.

Metal mesh arch formers

Arch formers
Expanded-metal arch formers are made in standard shapes and are easy to install. The shapes can be modified by adding a soffit strip.

Semi-circular

Oriental

Tudor

Spanish

Expanded metal mesh arch formers are available from builders' merchants to give quick and easy installation. Various profiles are made, typically semi-circles, corner quadrants and ellipses, although Spanish, Oriental and Tudor styles are also available.

One-piece mesh frames are also sold, but they're suitable only for use on 112mm (4½in) thick walls. Segmented formers – half the face and half the soffit (underside) – are more versatile; some offer a separate soffit strip to cope with any wall thickness.

Fitting the former
You'll need to wedge a batten at the top of the opening, to which you can attach the mesh with nails. Hold the former in position, and set it squarely using a spirit level **(1)**. Secure the mesh to the piers with galvanized masonry nails – you may have to hack off a margin of plaster at the sides so the mesh can be fixed flat against the bricks. Hold a spirit level diagonally against the fold of mesh at the curves and the hard plaster surface on the pier, to check that it's set at the correct depth **(2)**.

If you're fitting mesh segments, fit one half, then the other **(3)** and tie the soffit strips together with galvanized or copper wire to prevent the mesh sagging under the weight of the plaster. On a thick wall, insert a soffit strip and tie it to the side pieces.

Mix up some metal lathing plaster (◁) and spread a rough key coat onto the soffit with a plasterer's steel trowel, working from bottom to top from both sides **(4)**. Don't press too hard or the plaster will be forced through the mesh. Apply plaster to the face of the arch, scraping it off level with the hard plaster edge on the pier and the rigid mesh fold on the arch curve. When the plaster has stiffened, after about 15 minutes, apply a thin coat of ordinary finish plaster. Apply a second coat immediately after the first and trowel smooth.

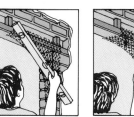

1 Set former square **2 Check it is level** **3 Tie former soffits** **4 Apply plaster**

Fibrous plaster arches

Prefabricated decorative archways are available made from fibrous plaster. They are usually fixed with screws to wooden battens at the top and sides of the opening. The joints between the fibrous plaster mouldings and the wall plaster are filled after installation.

To complete an authentic period look, ornate fibrous plaster accessories such as corbels (supporting brackets) or pillars and pilasters are also available with which to clad the piers.

MAKING A CUSTOMIZED ARCH

When you cannot find the arch profile you require as a pre-made former, make your own in one of two ways.

Using wet plaster
The arch may be a single curve, or may incorporate intricate curves and points. Cut 12mm (½in) plywood ribs to the contour of the arch shape but make them 12mm (½in) less than the finished size. Nail or screw them to the beam fixings and piers. Nail softwood spacer battens between the ribs.

Cut and fix expanded metal mesh sheeting across the faces and edge of the shape, moulding it around the curves **(1)**. You may have to snip the mesh with tinsnips to enable you to fold it around tight shapes.

Make up plastering guides from hardboard. Cut these to the finished shape you require. Temporarily nail them, smooth side inwards, over the mesh, with packing pieces behind. The packing should equal the finished thickness of the plaster. Set the edges of the guide to overlap the underside of the arch by 12mm (½in), the required thickness of plaster. Spread plaster onto the underside of the arch, between the overlapping edges. When this has set, remove the guides and plaster the wall faces using the hard plaster edge as a level. Finally apply finish plaster.

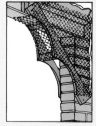

1 Fix mesh to ribs   **2 Fit plasterboard**

Using plasterboard
You can use plasterboard to make an arch to your own design. Cut the sheet to the required profile and nail it over the framework **(2)**. Cut a thin strip of hardboard or thin plywood for the soffit and pin it to the frame to form the underside of the arch. Fix the hardboard textured side out. Bed paper scrim in plaster over the joins to prevent cracking due to slight movement. Apply a skim coat of finish plaster to all the surfaces. Alternatively, pin a strip of metal mesh to the soffit and apply a base coat and finish coat of plaster.

REMOVING A NON-LOADBEARING WALL

Lightweight partition walls which are not loadbearing can be removed safely without consulting the authorities for approval, and without the need to add temporary supports. You must, however, be certain that the wall is in fact not structural before doing so, as some partitions do offer partial support.

Dismantling a stud partition

Remove the skirting boards from both sides of the wall, plus any picture rail mouldings: it's a good idea to save these for re-use or repairs in the future. If any electrical switches or socket outlets are attached to the wall, they must be disconnected and re-routed before work begins.

Removing the plasterwork
Use a claw hammer or wrecking bar to hack off the plaster and laths or plasterboard cladding covering the wall frame. Once stripped to the framework, remove the vertical studs. Bag up the debris during stripping and remove.

Removing the framework
First knock away any nailed noggings from between the studs. If the studs are nailed to the head and sill, they can be knocked apart. If they are housed or mortised in place, saw through them (at an angle to prevent the saw jamming). If you make the cut close to the joint, you will be left with a useful length of re-usable timber.

Prise off the head and sill members from the ceiling joists and floor. If the end studs are fixed to the walls, prise them away with a wrecking bar.

Finishing off
Replaster the gap in the ceiling and walls, fitting a narrow strip of plasterboard if necessary (▷). Fit floorboarding to close the gap if the boards are not continuous.

Dismantling a blockwork wall

Partition walls are sometimes made using lightweight concrete blocks. To remove the wall, start to cut away the individual units with a bolster chisel and club hammer from the top. Work from the middle out to the sides.

Chop off an area of plaster first, so that you can locate the joints between blocks, then drive your chisel into these to lever them out.

METHODS OF CLOSING A FLOOR GAP

When you remove a dividing wall that penetrates the floor, you are left with a gap between the floors on each side. The floorboards may run parallel with, or at right-angles to, the line of the wall. Filling the gap with new floorboards is straightforward.

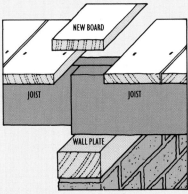

Boards running parallel
When the boards are parallel with the wall the supporting joists may rest on a wall plate (▷) built into the lower wall. Cut a board matching the thickness of the floorboards to fill the gap. Nail the board to the joists.

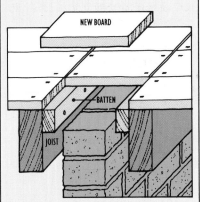

Boards at right-angles
When the boards are at right-angles to the gap, the ends will be supported on joists running parallel with the wall and about 50mm (2in) from it.

Cut the ends of the board flush with the joists. Nail 50 x 25mm (2 x 1in) sawn softwood battens to the sides of the joists level with the underside of the boards. Cut short lengths of matching floorboards to bridge the gap and nail them to the battens.

● **Making a room divider in an old house**
Create a room divider by stripping the plasterwork from the studding to reveal the timber framework. Once it is clean, paint or stain the frame to suit your interior decorative scheme.

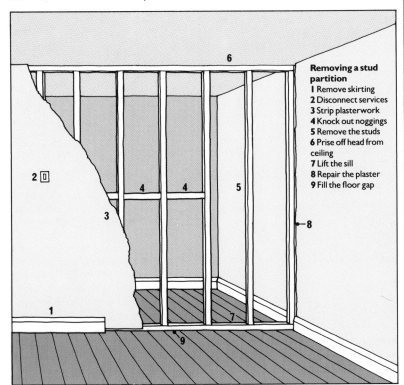

Removing a stud partition
1 Remove skirting
2 Disconnect services
3 Strip plasterwork
4 Knock out noggings
5 Remove the studs
6 Prise off head from ceiling
7 Lift the sill
8 Repair the plaster
9 Fill the floor gap

ALIGNING FLOORS

When the joists run parallel with a wall that's been removed (◁), you may find that one floor is out of level with the other. This may have been caused by slight movement in parts of the building or they may have been built that way; the floors were never intended to be aligned. Depending on the difference between floors, you can make a slope or step to deal with the unevenness satisfactorily.

Packing and trimming

When the joists of the two floors are supported on the same wall plate (◁), the chances are that both floors will be at the same level. Because wood can shrink or warp, however, it may be necessary to pack or trim the top of one or two joists slightly to allow for the infill board to sit properly.

Dealing with misalignment

A misalignment up to 18mm (¾in) can be accommodated by the short lengths of floorboards cut to span the gap. Although probably acceptable, the slope will be apparent. Where the difference in level is large, it may be necessary to create a single step or make a gradual slope. A gradual slope should be less noticeable, but cannot satisfactorily run across a door opening.

Making a step

Trim the ends of the floorboards on the high side flush with the joists and nail a batten to it. Trim the boards on the low side in the same way, but screw a 38mm (1½in) thick planed softwood riser to the side of the joist to finish level with the batten (See right).

If the floors are to be covered, cut and nail short lengths of floorboards to form the step tread. Where you want a bare wood floor, a single board running the width of the step would look better. In this case, skew-nail noggings flush with and between the riser and adjacent joists at approximately 750mm (2ft 6in) centres – necessary for a wide board that is weak across its width.

Where a floor has been raised, make a shallow threshold step at a doorway. Prepare a hardwood threshold board to fit between the door linings and finish flush with the raised floor. Nail it to the lower floor. Trim the bottom of the door to clear the step and refit it on its hinges (◁).

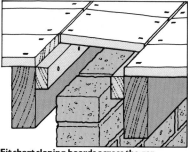

Fit short sloping boards across the gap

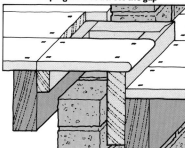

Make a step if difference in level is large

Fit a threshold at a doorway

MAKING A GRADUAL SLOPE

Cut the floorboards flush with the joist on the high side and nail a batten to it as before. Remove the skirting boards from the side walls and lift the floorboards of the room with the lower floor. Rest the edge of a straight-edged board on the nailed batten of the high floor and one of the joists of the lower floor to give a gradual slope. **(1)**

Take measurements between each joist and the underside of the straight-edged board. Set an adjustable bevel to the angle between the side of the joist and the board. Cut with a power saw lengths of 50mm (2in) wide softwood to these dimensions at the required angle. Nail the prepared packing to the top of the joists in descending order.

Re-lay the floorboards, butting their ends against the cut board of the higher floor. Adjust the lengths of the boards for extension pieces to be laid into the floor at their other ends. **(2)** For a finished wood floor, re-lay and stagger the boards of both floors to break up the straight joint line.

Replace the skirting following the line of the floor and re-nail to the wall.

Setting the slope
Measure gap between a straight-edged board and each joist and set an adjustable bevel to the angle. Cut packing strips to fit and nail in place, followed by the floorboard.

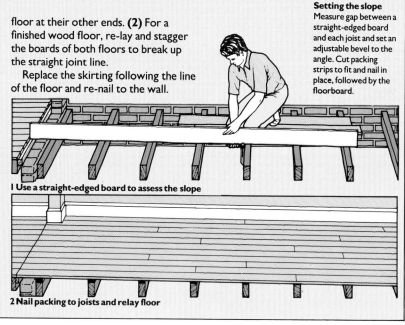

1 Use a straight-edged board to assess the slope

2 Nail packing to joists and relay floor

MAKING ONE ROOM INTO TWO

Building a partition to divide a large area into two smaller ones – to improve storage facilities, or simply because the house layout isn't as you'd like it – is quite straightforward using a frame of timber studs. You can clad the wall and plaster it so the new addition looks an integral part of the design. Before you can go ahead, however, you may need to seek approval.

Complying with the Regulations

Before you build a partition wall, check with your local council beforehand in order that the space you are creating complies with the Regulations.
These state that if a new room is to be 'habitable' – a living room, dining room, bedroom (but not a WC, bathroom or kitchen) – it must meet requirements, relating to ventilation.

The Regulations stipulate that an open space must be available on the outside of the window to provide sufficient ventilation to the room. The openable area of the windows to each room must be not less than a twentieth of the room's floor area. To check this, divide the area of the floor by the area of the window's sash or top vent. If the openable part is too small you may need to change the window.

Alternative and additional means of ventilation may be provided by a mechanical ventilator direct to the open air. It may be permissible for a fanlight to connect to a vented lobby.

If you plan to partition a large bedroom to make an en-suite shower or WC on an internal wall, natural light will not be required, but ventilation will. Consider the positioning of the new room in relation to the existing plumbing and the means of ventilation.

Should you plan to make a large bedroom into two smaller units, for example, bear in mind the size and shape of the rooms in relation to the furniture. Provide space around the bed to allow it to be made comfortably. You'll also need a corridor to make the two rooms self-contained.

Constructing a stud partition

Timber-framed non-loadbearing walls can be built relatively easily. The frame is usually made from 100 x 50mm (4 x 2in) or 75 x 50mm (3 x 2in) sawn softwood. The partition comprises: a head or ceiling plate, which forms the top of the wall and is fixed to the ceiling joists; a matching length, nailed to the floor, which forms the sill, or sole plate; studs which fit between the plates, equally spaced – about 400mm (1ft 4in) apart – and fixed with nails; short noggings which are nailed between the studs to make the structure rigid. Noggings will be needed where horizontal joints occur in the panelling.

Positioning the partition

If the new partition is run at right-angles to the floor and ceiling joists, it can be fitted at any point. Each joist will share the load and provide a solid fixing.

If the wall is to run parallel with the joists, it must stand directly over one of them: this may mean altering the overall dimensions of your planned rooms. Locate the floor joist in question and check whether stiffening is required. If so, reinforce it as described, which will require considerable work (▷).

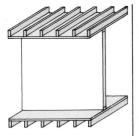

Right-angle
A partition set at right-angles to joists is well supported.

Parallel
A partition parallel with the joists must be supported by one of them.

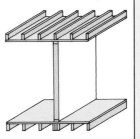

Reinforcing
The floor joist may need stiffening to bear the extra weight of the partition (See right).

REINFORCING A JOIST

Remove the skirting and lift the floorboards. Temporarily lay some of the boards to walk on while working. Screw metal joist hangers (▷) to the walls at each end, using 50mm (2in) long screws, to support the reinforcing joists flush with the original joist. Cut two reinforcing joists to fit between the hangers. Allow not more than 6mm (¼in) for tolerance.

Use 12mm (½in) diameter coachbolts to clamp the joists together. Drill the holes for them slightly larger than their diameter and spaced not more than 900mm (3ft) apart, working from the centre. Place large plain washers under the head and nut.

You can alternatively use 75mm (3in) diameter double-sided timber connectors between the meeting faces instead of joist hangers. If you have room, and a drill bit long enough, drill through all three joists while they are held together with cramps. If not, cramp one in place and drill through the two. Remove the reinforcing joist and cramp the other on the opposite side. Drill through it using the hole in the original joist as a guide. Bolt the reinforcing joists together.

Replace the floorboards on which to erect the partition (See below).

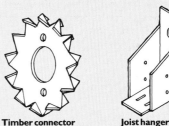

Timber connector   **Joist hanger**

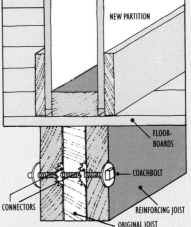

Stiffening the joist
Bolt a joist to each side of the original using coachbolts and timber connectors.

Parts of a stud partition
1 Head plate
2 Sole plate (sill)
3 Wall stud
4 Studs
5 Noggings

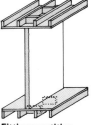

Fitting a partition between joists
Fit timber bearers between the floor joists and ceiling joists to support the stud partition.

21

BUILDING A STUD PARTITION

Making a stud partition wall is the easiest way to divide a room into two: you can construct a plain wall, or add a doorway, serving hatch or glazed area to 'borrow' light from an existing window. You can build the partition directly onto the floorboards, or the joists *below, so that the flooring can be independent of the partition, should you need to lift boards later. The sides of the partition can be set against the plaster surface or set in channels to provide a better fixing to the masonry and make any unevenness easier to fill.*

Marking out and spacing the studs

Mark the width of the sill for the new wall on the floor in chalk. Use the sill member – a length of 100 x 50mm (4 x 2in) sawn softwood – as a guide to draw the line. Continue the guidelines up the walls at each side, using a spirit level and straight-edged plank or a plumbline and bob. Continue the guidelines onto the ceiling, by snapping a distinct chalk line onto the surface with a taut string (1).

Spacing the studs
Lay the sill and head members together with their face sides uppermost. Mark the position of the studs at 400mm (1ft 4in) or 600mm (2ft) centres, working from the middle. Square the lines across both members against a try square (2). Use the 400mm (1ft 4in) spacing to support thin board materials and 9.5mm (⅜in) thick plasterboard.

If you are fixing 12.7mm (½in) plasterboard or tongued-and-grooved (T&G) boarding the 600mm (2ft) spacing should be used.

Marking out a doorway
If you are including a doorway in the wall, make an allowance for the width of the opening. The studs that form the sides of the opening must be spaced apart by the width of the door plus a 6mm (¼in) tolerance gap and the thickness of both door linings. Mark the width of the opening on the head plate at the required positions, then mark the positions for the studs working from the opening. Take the dimensions for the sill from the head and cut both plates to length (3). The door studs overlap the ends of the sills, which must be cut back to allow for them.

Fixing the framework

Secure the sill to the floor on each side of the door opening using 100mm (4in) long nails or 75mm (3in) long No. 10 countersunk woodscrews. Use the head plate as a guide to keep both parts of the sill in line.

Prop the head plate against the ceiling on its line and check the stud marks are true with the sill, using a plumbline. Nail or screw it to the joists (4).

Measure the distance between the head and sill at each end and cut the outer wall studs to length: they should be a tight fit between the sill and head plate. Drill and plug the walls if you're fixing the studs with screws, or use 75mm (3in) long masonry nails.

Fixing door studs
Cut the door studs to fit between the head plate and floor. Wedge them in place but do not fix them yet. Add together the door height and the thickness of the head lining, plus 10mm (⅜in) for tolerance, then mark the position of the underside of the door head on the edge of one stud. Hold a spirit level on this mark and transfer it accurately to the other door stud.

Fixing the door head
Remove the studs, then mark and cut a 12mm (½in) deep housing to receive the 50mm (2in) door head. Reposition and skew-nail the door studs to the head plate and dovetail-nail into the ends of the sills (◁). Locate the door head member in its housing and dovetail-nail it through the studs (5). Fit a short stud between the head plate and door head.

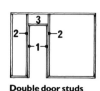

Double door studs
1 Door-height studs
2 Full-height studs
3 Door head

Alternative fixing for door studs

An alternative method for fixing the door studs is to cut the door studs to the required door height and double up with a stud between the sill and head plate. Support the door head and nail it to the top of the door studs. Cut a short length of studding to fit vertically between the centre of the head plate and door head. Secure in place by dovetail-nailing. Make sure when nailing all the parts together that their faces are flush.

1 Snap a chalk line onto the ceiling

2 Mark the sill and head plate together

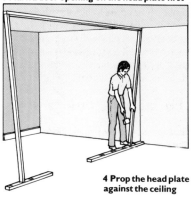

3 Mark a door opening on the head plate first

4 Prop the head plate against the ceiling

5 Nail the studs to the door head

STUD PARTITIONS

Fixing studs and noggings

Measure and cut each full length stud and fix in turn (See right). Cut the noggings to fit between the studs and, working from the wall, skew-nail the first end to the wall stud then dovetail-nail through the next stud into the end of the nogging. One or two rows of noggings may be required: if you are going to fit plasterboard horizontally, place the centre of the noggings at 1.2m (4ft), working from the ceiling. When the boards are to be fitted vertically, space the line of noggings evenly, staggering them to make the fixing easier.

Space studs equally and nail top and bottom

Nail noggings between studs to stiffen them

Fixing to an existing stud wall

Stud partitions are commonly used for internal walls of rooms on the first floor level. If your new partition meets a timber-framed wall, align it with the existing solid frame members.

Fix the wall stud of the new partition to a stud in the existing wall, where possible. Locate the stud by tapping, then drill a series of closely spaced holes through the plaster to find its centre.

When the new partition wall falls between the studs of the original one, fix its studs to the noggings, head and sill of the original wall. Construct the new wall as above but, in this instance, cut the wall stud to fit between the floor and the ceiling and fix it before the sill and head plate are nailed into place.

Fixing plasterboard vertically

Start at the doorway with the edge of the first board flush with the stud face. Before fixing, cut a 25mm (1in) wide strip, from the edge, down to the bottom edge of the door head member. Fix the board with 30mm (1¼in) or 40mm (1½in) plasterboard nails not more than 150mm (6in) apart. Fit the boards on both sides of the doorway then cut and fit a section over the opening. Allow a 3mm (⅛in) gap at the cut joint. Fit the remaining boards.

Fixing plasterboard horizontally

Plasterboard can be fitted horizontally where it is more economical or convenient to do so. First nail the top line of boards in place, so that, should it be necessary to cut the bottom run of boards, the cut edge will fall behind the skirting. Cut a strip from the edge of the boards on each side of the doorway to allow for the boarding over the door to be fixed to the studs.

Temporarily nail a horizontal support batten to the studs 3mm (⅛in) below the centre line of the noggings. Sit a board on the batten and nail it to the studs. Fit the remainder of the top boards in this way; then fit the bottom row. Stagger the vertical joints.

A second person should assist you by holding the plasterboard steady. If you have to work alone use a length of timber to prop the board while you work. Nail from the centre of the board.

NAILING TECHNIQUES

Use two 100mm (4in) round wire nails to skew-nail each butt joint, one through each side. Temporarily nail a batten behind the stud to prevent it moving sideways when driving in the first nail. Battens cut to fit between each stud can be permanently nailed in place to form housings for extra support.

Alternative stud fixing method

For a really rigid fixing, set the studs into 12mm (½in) deep housings notched into the head and sill plates before nailing.

Skew-nailing
Skew-nail the butt joints with two nails.

Nailing technique
Support the stud with a block while driving the first nail.

Supporting joint
Battens fixed to each side brace the joint.

Housing joints
Housing joints ensure a true and rigid frame.

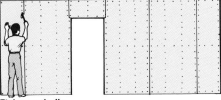

Fixing vertically
Work away from a doorway or start at one end.

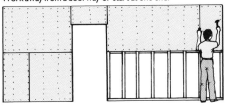

Fixing horizontally
Fix the top row first, stagger the joints on the next.

BUILDING A STAGGERED PARTITION

A stud wall can be built to divide a room into two and provide alcoves for storage at the same time. The method of construction is the same as described for the straight partition (◁) but also includes right-angle junctions. Constructing a staggered partition with a door at one end and a spacious alcove, as shown below, makes sensible use of available space.

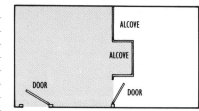

A staggered partition will form storage alcoves on each side, one for each room.

Building the wall
1 Mark out partitions
2 Transfer the marks to the ceiling
3 Cut and fix the sills to the floor
4 Fix the head plates to the ceiling
5 Make corners from three studs
6 Fix the other studs at required spacing
7 Fit noggings, then fix the boarding
8 Fit door frame and complete the boarding
9 Fit door lining, door and mouldings

Positioning the wall

Mark out the thickness of the main partition across the floor. Mark the position of the 'recessed' partition parallel with it. For clothes storage set them apart by 600mm (2ft).

Calculate the length of the partitions by setting them out on the floor. Starting from the wall adjacent to the doorway measure off the thickness of a stud, the door lining, the width of the

door, a second door lining and a second stud. Also add 6mm (¼in) for clearance around the door. This takes you to the face of the first short partition that runs parallel to the wall. Measure from this point to the other wall and divide the dimension in two. This gives you the line for the other short partition. Set out their thicknesses at right angles to the main partitions.

Fixing the sill and head plates

Mark the positions for the head plates on the ceiling. Use a straight edge and spirit level or a plumbline to ensure that the marks exactly correspond with those marked on the floor.

Cut and fix the sill and head plates to the floor and ceiling respectively, as for erecting a straight partition. Cut and fit the studs at the required spacing to suit the thickness of the cladding.

CONSTRUCTING THE CORNERS

The right-angled corners and the end of the short partition, which supports the door frame, need extra studs to provide a fixing for the plasterboard.

Make up a corner from three studs arranged and nailed in place. Fit short off-cuts of studding to pack out the gap. Fix the offcuts level with the noggings. Fit the boards with one edge overlapping the end of the adjoining panel. For the end of the short partition fit two studs spaced 50mm (2in) apart with nailed offcuts between. Nail the board to the two faces of the partition. Leave the end exposed until the door frame is fitted.

Measure and cut the door studs, ceiling and door head plates to length. Nail the ceiling head in place and fix one stud to the room wall and one to the stud wall. Ensure they are square and flush with the end of the partition. Fit the door head plate and a short vertical stud above it. Plasterboard over the doorway and to the side faces of the studs, including the end of the wall.

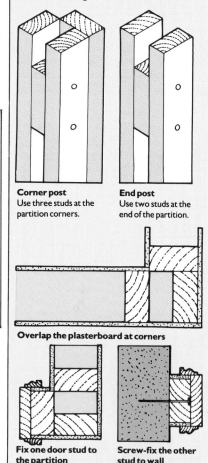

Corner post
Use three studs at the partition corners.

End post
Use two studs at the end of the partition.

Overlap the plasterboard at corners

Fix one door stud to the partition

Screw-fix the other stud to wall

Unlike solid walls of brick or block, stud walls are mainly hollow, presenting problems when wall fixtures are to be hung. Wherever possible these should be fixed directly to the structural stud members for maximum support, but if the positions of fixtures are pre-planned, extra studding, noggings or mounting boards can be incorporated before the wall lining is applied.

Mounting a hand basin

A wall-mounted hand basin will need a sound enough fixing to carry its own weight and that of someone leaning on it when it is in use.

Buy the basin before building the wall – or work from the manufacturer's literature, which usually specifies the distance between centres for fixing the brackets – and position two studs to take the fixing screws. Mark the centre lines of the studs on the floor before applying the wall lining, then draw plumbed lines from the marks up the face of the lining. Measure the height from the floor for the brackets and fix them securely with wood screws.

If you plan wall-mounted taps above the basin make a plywood mounting board to fit between a pair of standard spaced studs to carry both the basin and the taps. Use exterior grade plywood at least 18mm (¾in) thick. Plywood is tougher and more stable than softwood and chipboard doesn't hold screws well.

Screw 50 x 50mm (2 x 2in) battens to the inside faces of the studs, set back from their front edges by the thickness of the board. Cut the board to size with enough height to support basin and taps, then screw it to the battens to lie flush with the two studs.

Apply the lining to the side of the wall that will carry the basin, leaving the other side open for plumbing in the appliances. Drill clearance holes and fit the taps; fix the basin support brackets, preferably with bolts.

To hide the plumbing within the wall pass the waste downpipe through a hole drilled in the wall sill member and run it under the floor. If the waste pipe must run sideways in the wall, notch the studs (See below).

Fitting a wall cupboard

It is not always possible to fix in the studding because walls tend to be put up well before furnishings are considered. If there are no studs just where you want them you will have to use cavity fixings instead. Choose a type that will adequately support the unit (See right).

Hanging shelving

Wall-mounted bookshelves have to carry a considerable weight and must be fixed securely, especially to stud partitions. Use a shelving which has strong metal uprights into which adjustable brackets are slotted. The uprights spread the load across all the wall fixings. Screw into studs if you can; otherwise use suitable cavity fixings (See below right).

Hanging small fixtures

Load-carrying fixtures with a small contact area can crush the plaster and strain the fixings. Mount coat hooks, for instance, on a board to spread the load and screw the boards to studs. Hang small pictures on picture hooks secured with steel pins, larger ones on a double pin type, preferably fixed to a stud. Put mirror plates on the frame of a heavy mirror or picture for screw fixing. Use stranded wire if hanging them on a hook fixed to a stud or a cavity fixing.

SEE ALSO

Details for: ▷
Plumb line | 76

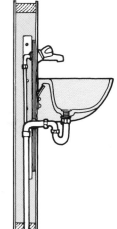

Mounting a basin ▶
Fix a wall-mounted hand basin and taps to an exterior-grade plywood board.

FITTING SERVICES IN STUD PARTITIONS

It is easy to plan and fit services in a stud partition wall before lining it. To guard against future occupants drilling into service runs set horizontal cables or pipes no more than 300mm (12in) above floor level.

Plumbing
Plan the runs of supply or waste pipes by marking the faces of the vertical studs or the noggings that brace them. Remember that a waste pipe must have a slight fall. When you are satisfied with the layout, cut notches in the timbers for the pipework (See right).

Transfer the marked lines to the sides of the studs or noggings and drill holes for the pipes close to their front edges. Cut in to the holes to make notches. If cut at a slight angle they will hold the pipes while they are being fitted.

Notches cut for waste pipes must be reinforced to prevent them weakening the studs. Drill the holes in the centres of the studs, following the pipe run.

Before cutting in to the holes cut housings for 300mm (12in) lengths of 50 x 25mm (2 x 1in) softwood to bridge the notches. Make the notches, set the waste pipe in place, then screw the bridging pieces into their housings flush with the fronts of the studs.

Noggings need not be braced, but fit one under a pipe bend as a support.

Running electric cable
Drill 12 to 18mm (½ to ¾in) holes at the centres of the studs for level runs of cable and in noggings for vertical runs. Fit extra noggings to carry mounting boxes for sockets and switches. For a flush-mounted fitting inset the board to the depth of the box so that its front edge lies flush with the lining. Run the cable. With the lining in place mark and cut an opening for the box and pull the cable through. If you have omitted a mounting board during construction, you can use dry-wall fixing flanges to hold the metal box to the lining.

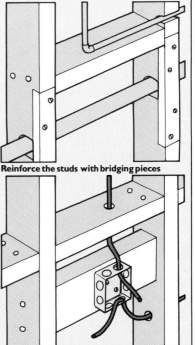

Reinforce the studs with bridging pieces

Fit metal boxes to a mounting board

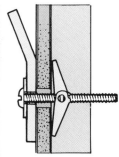

Spring-toggle fixing

Cavity fixings
Various cavity fixings may be had for insertion into holes and securing with screws or bolts. Some expand to grip the lining as a screw is tightened; some are held in place by a toggle that springs out behind the lining.

BUILDING A DRY PARTITION WALL

For a lightweight non-loadbearing partition, cellular-core dry partitioning is easy to construct. Made from two sheets of plasterboard with a cardboard core (◁), it makes a rigid wall when installed. The panels can be purchased from larger builders' merchants but would probably need to be ordered. Tapered-edged panels for decorating and square-edged panels for plastering are available. The panels provide a reasonable level of sound insulation, but as air gaps can reduce their performance an acoustic sealant can be applied to all the jointing surfaces during erection.

Fixing the framing

The panels are fixed to a lightweight timber frame. Mark out the floor, walls and ceiling in the same way as for a stud partition. Nail to the floor a 50mm (2in) planed (PAR) softwood sill, which matches the thickness of the partitioning. Plane 18mm (¾in) thick softwood ceiling and perimeter wall battens to make a snug fit in the gap between the plasterboard sheets. Remove the arris from the outside long edges of the battening and then nail or screw it to the wall. To locate the bottom of the partition cut a point on a 150mm (6in) length of the ceiling/wall batten and nail it to the sill with its square end against the wall batten. Use 50mm (2in) wall nails.

Fixing the panels

Cut the panels to fit between the sill and the ceiling with a 3mm (⅛in) tolerance using a saw. Rip out the cardboard core with the claw of a hammer to the depth of the battens – about 18mm (¾in) – along the top and two long edges. Also remove 150mm (6in) of the core from each end of the bottom edge. Use a wood chisel to trim away any lumps of glue.

Drive a 150mm (6in) length of battening into the core at the bottom of the partitioning. This plug is used to fix skirtings – add more approximately 400mm (1ft 4in) apart. Mark the position of each on the surface of the partition for reference later.

Lift and locate the top of the first panel over the ceiling batten about 200mm (8in) from the wall. Swing the panel into the vertical position and locate it on the floor sill. Slide the panel carefully along the sill to locate over the locating block and wall batten. Cut an intermediate locating block 300mm (1ft) long and taper each end. Tap half of its length into the bottom corner of the panel's core and nail it to the sill.

Cut a length of square-section vertical joint batten to fit between the ceiling batten and intermediate block. Tap the batten half way into the edge of the panel. Skew-nail it at the top and bottom. Fix the boards to the framework with galvanized nails at 225mm (9in) centres (◁).

Prepare the other panels and secure them in the same way. Butt the edges of the tapered panels, but leave a 3mm (⅛in) gap when they are square-edged.

Partition components
1 Softwood sill at base of panel
2 Wall batten (hidden inside long edge of panel)
3 Ceiling batten
4 Locating block (hidden)
5 Cellular-core panel
6 Intermediate locating block
7 Vertical joint batten

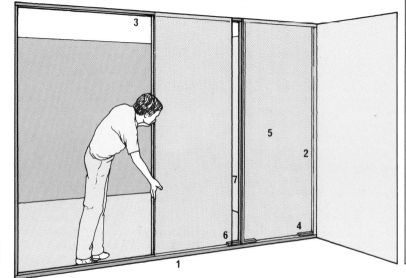

JOINTS AND JUNCTIONS

Joints

To make a T-joint, nail a vertical wall batten to one of the joint battens or to plugs cut from the joint battening and driven into the core of the corresponding partition. Fit the 150mm (6in) long plugs horizontally, spaced about 600mm (2ft) apart, before erecting the partition. Hammer them into the edge, following a line of cells. Use a spare length of battening to drive the plugs further in from the edge if required. Always mark the position of the plugs on the surface.

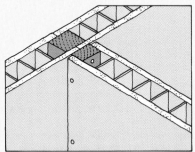

Fixing to joint batten

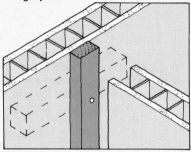

Junctions

Right–angle corners are made by cutting away the inside face of the plasterboard and core to form a rebate for the full width of the adjoining panel. A batten must be fitted into each panel for nailing.

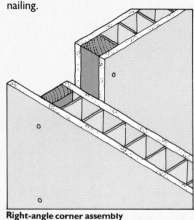

Right-angle corner assembly

Making a door opening

Mark the position of the doorway on the floor. Make allowances for the width of the door and door linings (▷). Mark out the width of the panels, working from the opening to each wall. Fit the ceiling and wall battens. Cut the sill to stop at the opening and fix it to the floor. Fit the panels working from the wall towards the opening, starting with any cut panels. At the opening, remove the core from the vertical edges of the panels and insert vertical battens flush wih the edges. Skew-nail them at top and bottom and fix the plasterboard with galvanized nails at 225mm (9in) intervals.

Measure and cut a panel to fit over the door opening. Nail a length of wall batten with one end tapered to the side of the vertical batten on each side of the opening. The battens should be about 75mm (3in) shorter than the depth of the cut panel: Ensure they are set true.

Clear the core from all round the panel, allowing enough room at the bottom to accommodate a length of joint battening. Slide the panel over the side battens and nail it in place with a 3mm (⅛in) gap at the top.

Fit the horizontal head batten into the core flush with the bottom edge and nail it to the vertical battens at each end, then nail the door linings to the stud framework.

If you fit a made-up door frame, treat it as a panel and build it in as the other partitions are erected. When assembling the partition, don't forget to omit a section of the sill at the doorway.

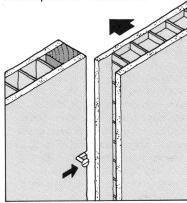
Slide the panel over the side battens

Fitting a partition between walls

Working from one wall mark out the width of the full panels across the floor. Inevitably, you will have to cut the last panel to fit. Measure and cut it to the required width, less 6mm (¼in). Fix the framing to the floor, ceiling and both walls. Fit the bottom locating batten.

Prepare and fit the cut panel at one end and then proceed from each end towards the centre. Clean out the core from the panels on each side of the opening to allow the jointing batten to be set in flush. Make three equally spaced wide saw cuts in the edge of the panels. Cut the vertical battens so that they fit loosely between the ceiling batten and sill. Set them flush into the prepared edges of the panel. Fit 50mm (2in) screws part way into the centre of the battens at each of the saw cuts. Lift the last panel into position, then tap the screws sideways to drive half the vertical batten into the edge of the last panel. Skew-nail the vertical batten to the top and bottom frames through the board. Fix the panels along the vertical edges.

Insert last panel then tap batten sideways

SEE ALSO

Details for: ▷	
Door casings	61, 64
Wall flanges	78

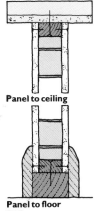

Fixing details

Panel to ceiling

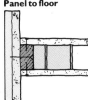

Panel to floor

Panel to wall

FITTING FIXTURES AND INSTALLING SERVICES

Fixtures
Lightweight loads such as pictures, clocks and display shelving may be fitted with cavity wall fixings. Heavy loads such as shelving or storage units should be screwed to wooden plugs installed into the core before assembly. Shelving systems with metal uprights can be screwed to the plugs. A surface-mounted board screwed to a pair of plugs will help to spread the load of a heavy cabinet.

Services
Electric cable can be passed horizontally through the centre of the core as the panels are erected. Use a 25mm (1in) diameter pipe to clear a path for the cable. A permanent length of plastic conduit running through the core may help you to feed the cable through as the panels are fitted. Vertical cable runs can be made providing they occur next to a joint in the panel.

Accurately cut an opening in the face of the partitioning for a switch or socket mounting box, and fit them with partition wall flanges (▷).

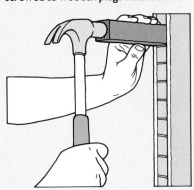
Drive wooden plugs in from the edge

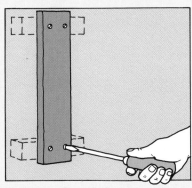
Fix mounting boards for heavy loads

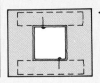
◄ Mounting boxes
Plugs can also be employed for fixing mounting boxes in the core cavity.

CEILINGS: LOWERING A CEILING

From a practical point of view, a high ceiling can be a liability. It incurs greater heating bills, and decorating costs will be higher as more material is required to cover the walls. Lowering the ceiling can help solve these problems as well as providing a distinctive feature in a room.

High ceilings are generally found in older types of house. Some are decorative moulded ceilings, while many others have simpler but attractive cornice mouldings and these should be preserved to maintain the character of the house. But where a room is plain and the ceiling needs attention, or where the proportions of the room would benefit from alteration, a lowered ceiling can be an improvement. It can be used to hide ducting, improve sound and heat insulation and provide a space for flush or concealed lights.

Changing the character of a room
A room's character is largely determined by the relation of its area to its ceiling height. Low cottage ceilings are considered charming and cosy, while tall rooms are felt to be very imposing, though they are usually larger all round. Other high-ceilinged rooms feel somehow rather 'uncomfortable'.

The sense of cosiness or emptiness may be based on practical experience. For example, the volume of a cottage room is less than that of a high-ceilinged room of the same floor area, so it would be easier to heat evenly, and a room with an even temperature feels more comfortable than one where the temperature varies due to rising air currents. The acoustics in a small room may also be better, inducing a relaxed feeling. Yet the qualities of light and space in a room may be due to its high ceiling, and if it were lowered, changing the room's proportions, the tall windows might look awkward and the sense of space be lost.

Making a model
Making a simple card model of a room's interior is a good way to check that a planned project will suit the room before spending time and money on the real thing.

Measure the length, width and height of the room and the height, width and positions of the windows and doors. Mark out and cut pieces of stiff card for the floor and walls to a scale of 1:10 (1mm = 1cm) or, in the imperial

measure, 1:12 (1in = 1ft).

Mark the positions of the doors and windows on the cardboard walls and cut out the openings with a craft knife. The openings will allow light into the finished model. You can hinge the 'door' in place with self-adhesive tape. Draw lines on the walls to represent the skirting and the architraves round the doors and windows. You can colour these details to make them more realistic. Also mark in the fireplace to the same scale. A projecting chimney breast can be easily formed in card and glued on.

Punch a small peep-hole in each wall at a height scaled to your eye level and assemble the floor and walls, using adhesive or sticky tape.

Cut a cardboard panel, representing the ceiling, to fit closely between the walls. If the real ceiling is to be the suspended type, with lighting round its edges, cut the panel smaller to provide the gap at the sides.

Cut two strips of card about 50mm (2in) wide and as long as the width of the ceiling piece and glue them on edge across the back of the 'ceiling'. Cut two more strips, the same width but a little longer, and use clips to attach these to the shorter ones. The longer strips will rest across the walls and the clips are adjusted to set the card ceiling at various heights. Check the effect of this on the room by viewing the interior space through the peepholes and the door and window openings.

To simulate a grid-system illuminated ceiling make a framework with strips of balsa wood to the same scale as the room and covered with tracing paper.

RECOMMENDED DIMENSIONS

The height of a new ceiling should be no less than 2.3m (7ft 6in). In some cases 2m (6ft 6in) is acceptable under beams or bay windows.

You can construct a slightly lower ceiling in a kitchen, provided at least half of it is at, or above, 2.3m (7ft 6in).

In a roof space the ceiling height must be a minimum of 2.3m (7ft 6in) for at least half the area of the room. However, this area might not represent the whole floor. Mark all the sloping ceilings 1m (3ft 3in) or 1.5m (5ft) above the floor, then use a plumbline to mark the floor directly below. The area of the floor within the marked lines represents the actual area used to calculate the ceiling height.

Set out the area on the floor

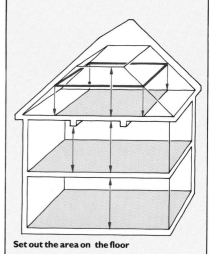

Cardboard model parts
1 Walls
2 Chimney breast
3 Floor
4 Ceiling panel
5 Fixed card strip
6 Adjustable card strip
7 Clips

Making a model
Construct a simple card model to help you visualize the final room proportions.

LOWERING A CEILING: OPTIONS

You might decide to lower a ceiling for practical reasons or simply to change the style of the interior, but whatever the reason, you should consider your options carefully because a ceiling is a large area which can be costly to cover.

Timber-framed ceilings are heavy but they can be tailor-made to suit the style and shape of a room using basic woodworking skills.

Manufactured suspended ceiling systems are relatively lightweight, easy to install and offer a wide choice of materials for the panelling, but a strong grid pattern is unavoidable.

Use the chart to help you consider the project in advance and to compare one system with another.

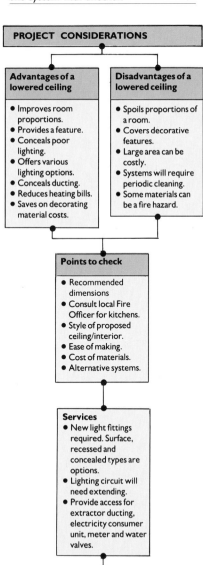

LOWERED CEILING

Design features	Planning the scheme	Type of construction	Covering/finishes
Will change the room proportions. Will hide old ceiling or services. Least likely to appear a conversion. Can be fitted with cornice mouldings. Without a hatch, prevents access to the void above.	Make initial sketches of the proposed interior, then draw scale plans on graph paper to detail and cost the scheme. Make a scale model to visualize the effect of the ceiling.	This type of construction uses new ceiling joists to span room in shortest direction. The joists are notched over battens fixed to the walls. Ties and hangers are used for spans over 2.4m (8ft).	Materials: Plasterboard. Fire-resistant building board. Veneered board. Tongued and grooved boarding. Mineral-fibre tiles. Finishes; papered, painted, varnished or ready-finished

PART-LOWERED CEILING

Design features	Planning the scheme	Type of construction	Covering/finishes
Similar to the full lowered ceiling above but has added interest of the split-level. The end 'drop' can be vertical or sloped, the latter being preferable when parallel with a window.	As for lowered ceiling (See above). Consider the line of the 'drop' in relation to the window. It should not cut across the window when viewed from the opposite side of the room.	Timber-frame construction as for lowered ceiling (See above). The end framework is formed from ties and hangers. The hangers are set at an angle for a sloped end.	As for lowered ceiling (See above).

SLATTED CEILING

Design features	Planning the scheme	Type of construction	Covering/finishes
Not a true ceiling but a framework which appears to be continuous. Most effective in hallways or passage. It does not seal off the old ceiling. Can be dismantled for access to services.	As for lowered ceiling (See above). The spacing and depth of the slats can be varied: you should not be able to see between the slats when looking straight ahead.	Edge-on plank construction using no sub-structure. Perimeter planks are housed and fixed to the wall; the slats are slotted into them.	No covering is used. The ceiling and walls above the slats are painted a dark colour. Finish for woodwork: Light-coloured stain, clear varnish or paint.

SUSPENDED CEILING

Design features	Planning the scheme	Type of construction	Covering/finishes
Appears to be suspended away from the walls and appears to float: concealed lighting enhances this illusion. Has modern character. Will mask old ceiling or services. Not demountable.	As for lowered ceiling (See above). Locate original ceiling joists and set out their position on your plan drawing: design the structure around them.	Timber-frame construction using ties fixed across ceiling joists and carrying hangers from which the new frame is suspended. The main components are assembled with bolts.	As for lowered ceiling (See above).

SUSPENDED CEILING SYSTEMS

Design features	Planning the scheme	Type of construction	Covering/finishes
A grid system manufactured from lightweight materials for self-assembly. Individual translucent or opaque panels sit in the grid framework. The system is demountable.	As for lowered ceiling (See above). Draw a plan of the room on graph paper and set out a symmetrical grid.	Lightweight aluminium T-sectioned bearers suspended from angle sections screwed to the walls. Bearers are loose fitted.	Metal: anodized. Panel materials: plain, textured and coloured translucent plastic; opaque plastic; mineral fibre.

SEE ALSO

Details for: ▷
Making a hatch   33

Vapour checks
Provide a vapour check to prevent condensation problems in an unventilated space above a lowered ceiling. Use a vapour-check plasterboard, an impervious sealer or polythene sheeting. The gaps between the boards or the polythene must be sealed effectively.

Plasterboard
Bed joints in mastic

Polythene sheeting
Fold and staple edges

29

CONSTRUCTING A LOWERED CEILING

You can build the new ceiling at any height providing it complies with the regulations. However, the height of window openings may limit your choice. About 2.4m (8ft) is a useful height for a lowered ceiling. It is a common room height for modern houses and relates to standard wallboard sheet sizes. Most manufacturers of built-in furniture adopt it as a standard height for ceilings.

Planning the layout

Making a lowered ceiling requires a considerable amount of timber for the framework and boarding to cover it. Work out your material requirements by drawing a plan to establish the most economical way to construct it. If you intend to use plasterboard choose a vapour-check type. Arrange the panels with the paper-covered edges set at right angles to the timber supports. Stagger the end joints between each row of boards and arrange them so as to fall on a joist.

If you plan to use tongued and grooved boarding, buy it in lengths that can be economically cut to suit your joist arrangement, as short off-cuts are wasteful. Avoid butt joints coinciding on adjacent boards.

Materials for the framework

Make a cutting list of the materials you will need to make up the structure. Use 75 x 50mm (3 x 2in) sawn softwood for the ceiling joists. These should span the room in the shortest direction. Calculate the number of joists you will need. These should be spaced at 400mm (1ft 4in) or 600mm (2ft) centres according to the thickness of the plasterboard. (◁). These dimensions will also suit other types of boarding.

You will need extra joist timber for the noggings fitted between the joists (◁). In addition 50 x 25mm (2 x 1in) sawn softwood is used for wall battens to run round the perimeter of the room.

Spans of over 2.4m (8ft) should be supported by hangers and ties, made from timber not less than 50 x 50mm (2 x 2in) which are fixed to the ceiling above. Place the hangers about the middle of the joists' span.

It is possible to use more hangers and reduce the section of the joists from 75 x 50mm (3 x 2in) to 50 x 50mm (2 x 2in). In this case place the hangers about 1m (3ft) apart.

Cutting list
A cutting list is your shopping guide. It will enable you to establish your requirements and help your supplier in making up your order. List the individual parts of the structure, and, under separate columns, fill in the quantity, length, width, thickness and material, required.

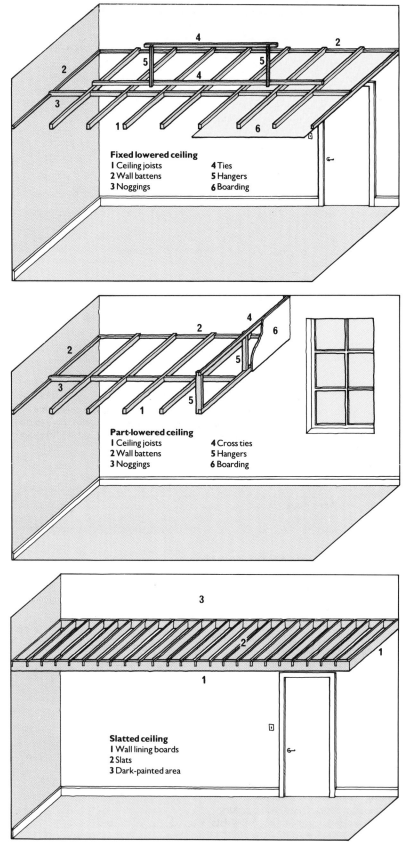

Fixed lowered ceiling
1 Ceiling joists	4 Ties
2 Wall battens	5 Hangers
3 Noggings	6 Boarding

Part-lowered ceiling
1 Ceiling joists	4 Cross ties
2 Wall battens	5 Hangers
3 Noggings	6 Boarding

Slatted ceiling
1 Wall lining boards
2 Slats
3 Dark-painted area

MAKING A SUSPENDED CEILING

Constructing the ceiling

Mark the height of the new ceiling, including the thickness of the boarding, on one wall. At this level draw a horizontal line across the wall using a straightedge and spirit level for accuracy. Continue the line around the room at this height. Cut the 50 x 25mm (2 x 1in) wall battens to length. Nail or screw them to the walls at 400mm (1ft 4in) intervals, with the bottom edge level with the line.

Cut the 75 x 50mm (3 x 2in) ceiling joists to length. Notch the ends to sit over the wall battens to bring the bottom edges flush. Skew-nail the joists to the wall battens. Cut and fit hangers and ties to prevent long joists sagging (See left). These supports also stiffen the structure.

Cut and nail noggings between the joists to support the edges of the plasterboard. Nail tapered-edge plasterboard to the joists, noggings and wall battening. Fill and tape the joints between boards and walls (▷).

Lowering part of a ceiling

You can lower part of a ceiling to overcome problems around tall window openings or to create a split-level effect. Follow the method for constructing a ceiling as described above but enclose the end drop with plasterboard nailed to hangers fixed in a line to a cross-tie member set above the last joist.

Making a slatted ceiling

Planed softwood planks 150 x 25mm (6 x 1in) in size, set on edge and spaced apart can create a simple yet effective slatted ceiling. Smaller sections can be used where the span is short, as with a narrow hallway.

Cut four lengths of planking to line the walls all round. Before nailing or screwing them at the required height, mark and cut housings in two of the planks opposite one another. Space the housings 225mm (9in) apart. For boards less than 150mm (6in) wide, space them about 100 to 150mm (4 to 6in) apart. Cut notches in the ends of the 'slat' boards to sit in the housings so that the bottom edges finish flush.

Before fitting the slats, paint walls and ceilings above the lining boards with a dark emulsion paint. Also paint ducting or plumbing to disguise it. Finish the slats with varnish, stain or paint.

A suspended ceiling is a framed panel which appears to float away from the walls. Fluorescent lights can be placed around the edge of the panel to enhance the floating effect and provide wall-washing illumination. The panel can be covered with plasterboard, decorative veneered ply or mineral-fibre ceiling tiles.

Locate the position of the ceiling joists by noting the direction of the floorboards of the room above; the joists will run at right angles to them (▷). Pinpoint the joists from below by drilling or boring pilot holes through the ceiling (▷). Mark the centre of each joist.

Setting out the grid
Measure the lengths of the walls and draw a scaled plan of the room on graph paper. Set out the shape of the ceiling panel on the drawing with its edges approximately 200mm (8in) from each wall. Then set out the position of the 50 x 50mm (2 x 2in) softwood ceiling ties. The ties should run at right angles to the joists of the ceiling above. The ends of the ties and sides of the two outer ones should be about 300mm (1ft) from the walls. The number of ties you'll need will depend on the size of the ceiling, but three should be a minimum. They should be spaced not more than 1m (3ft) apart for adequate support.

Constructing the ceiling
Counterbore and securely screw the ties in position to each of the joists they cross. Cut 50 x 50mm (2 x 2in) softwood hangers to the required length and fix

them to the ties with coach bolts not more than 1m (3ft) apart.

Cut additional ties to the same length as the planned ceiling panel. Bolt them across the ends of the hangers with an equal space at each end.

Cut the required number of 50 x 50mm (2 x 2in) planed softwood furring battens to suit the spacings necessary to support the boardings or tiles used as a covering. The length of the furring battens should be equal to the width of the ceiling panel less two 50 x 25mm (2 x 1in) capping battens. Equally space and screw the furring battens to the tie members. Countersink the screw heads.

Mark off the positions of the furring battens along the sides of each capping batten. Drive 75mm (3in) nails into, but not quite through, the cappings at these points. Apply woodworking adhesive and nail the cappings to the ends of the furring battens.

Finishing the assembly
Have electrical wiring installed in readiness for the fluorescent lights to be fitted. Cover the underside of the frame with plasterboard, decorative veneered boarding or ceiling tiles. Fill and flush the surface and edges of a plasterboard ceiling panel. Finish the exposed edges of the wooden frame to match the other materials as required.

Wire up and fit slim fluorescent light fittings to loose boards, which sit on top of the projecting frame. The fittings can then be easily removed for servicing at any time. Leave enough spare flex to allow the lights to be lifted clear.

SEE ALSO
Details for: ▷
Locating joist 33
Plasterboard 46–47

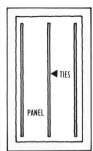
Setting out
Set out the panel on graph paper with a 200mm (8in) gap all round. Inset the ties about 300mm (1ft).

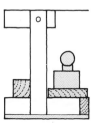
Light fitting
Fix a fluorescent light to a removable board for servicing.

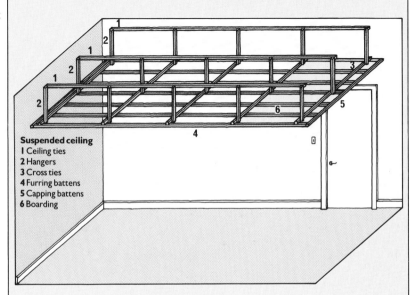
Suspended ceiling
1 Ceiling ties
2 Hangers
3 Cross ties
4 Furring battens
5 Capping battens
6 Boarding

31

SUSPENDED CEILING SYSTEMS

Manufactured suspended ceiling systems are made from slim metal sections, which provide a fairly lightweight structure for acoustic or translucent panels. They're quick and easy to fit using no specialist tools.

Panel layouts

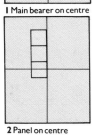

1 Main bearer on centre

2 Panel on centre

3 Cross bearer centred

4 Panel on centre

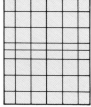

5 Best grid arrangement

Manufactured systems
Manufacturers offer a choice of coloured framing as well as coloured translucent and opaque panels.

The lightweight alloy framework is made from three basic elements: an angle section, which is fixed to the walls; a main bearer section, which spans the room, usually in the shortest direction; and a lighter T-sectioned cross bearer, which bridges the space between the main bearers.

The loose panels sit on the flanges provided by the bearers. They can be easily lifted out for access to ducting or to service light fittings, which can be concealed behind them. You need at least 200mm (4in) above the framework to fit the panels.

Setting out the grid

Normally, 600mm (2ft) square panels are used for suspended ceiling systems. Before fitting the framework, draw a plan of the ceiling on squared graph paper to ensure that the borders are symmetrical. Draw a plan of the room with two lines taken from the halfway point on each wall to bisect at the centre. Lay out the grid on your plan with a main bearer centred on the short bisecting line (**1**), then lay it out again with a line of panels centred on the same line (**2**). Use the grid that provides the widest border panels.

Plot the position of the cross bearers in the same way, using the other line (**3,4**). Try to get the border panels even on opposite sides of the room (**5**).

Fitting the framework

Before building a suspended ceiling with translucent panels, remove flaking materials and make good any cracks in the plaster ceiling above. Paint the ceiling with white emulsion to improve reflectivity if concealed fluorescent lighting is to be used.

Fix fluorescent light fittings to the joists spaced evenly across the ceiling: 16 watts per square metre is recommended for a suitable level of light in most rooms.

Mark the height of the suspended ceiling on the walls with a continuous levelled line. Hacksaw two lengths of wall angle section to fit the longest walls. Remove burrs from the ends with a file. Drill screw holes at 600mm (2ft) intervals. Drill and plug the walls using the angle as a guide and screw the components in place (**1**).

Next cut lengths of wall angle to fit the shorter walls. Their ends should fit on the angles already fitted. Screw-fix them in the same way.

Mark the positions of the bearers along two adjacent walls, as set out on the graph paper. Cut the main bearers

to span the room. Sit them on the wall angles (**2**). Use a ceiling panel to check they are parallel and at right angles to the wall and each other.

Cut the border cross bearers to fit between the end main bearers and wall angles. Set them in line with the points marked on the wall. Position the remainder of the cross bearers following the same line.

Working from the centre, drop in the full-sized panels. Measure and cut the border panels to fit and then drop them into place.

Spanning wide rooms
If the size of the room exceeds the maximum length of the main bearer, join two or more pieces together. A joint bridging piece is provided if the ends of the bearers are not made to lock together.

For spans exceeding 3m (10ft) support the main bearers with wire hangers. Fix each wire, spaced not more than 1.5m (5ft) apart, through a hole in the bearer and hang it from a screw eye in a furring strip or joist in the ceiling.

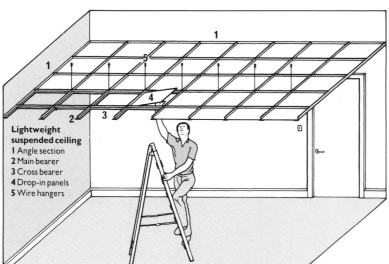

Lightweight suspended ceiling
1 Angle section
2 Main bearer
3 Cross bearer
4 Drop-in panels
5 Wire hangers

1 Screw the angle to the wall

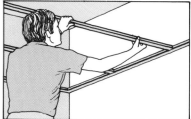

2 Position the main bearers

INSTALLING A FOLDING LOFT LADDER

Access to the roof space is more convenient and safer if you install a folding loft ladder. Some are complete with built-in hatch cover, frame and fittings ready to install in a new opening. Normally, the length of the ladders suits ceiling heights 2.3 and 2.5m (7ft 6in and 8ft 3in). Some can extend to 2.9 to 3m (9ft 6in to 10ft).

Concertina ladder
To fit a concertina ladder, securely screw the fixing brackets of the aluminium ladder to the framework of the opening. Fit the retaining hook to the framework to support the ladder in the stowed position. Operate the ladder with a pole, which hooks over the bottom rail. Fit the hatch door to the frame with a continuous hinge, followed by a push-to-release latch fixed to the edge of the hatch door.

Ready-to-install folding ladder
Cut the opening and trim the joists to the size specified by the manufacturer. Insert the casing with built-in frame in the opening and screw it to the joists.

A concertina ladder is simple to install.

Folding ladders are easy to deploy.

MAKING A LOFT ACCESS HATCH

Many houses are provided with a hatch in the ceiling to give access to the roof space for servicing water tanks and maintaining the roof structure. Should your house have a large roof space without access, installing a hatch could provide you with extra room for storage. Although the job is basically straightforward, it does entail cutting into the roof structure.

In older houses this is not a problem as the timbers are substantial. In modern houses, however, lightweight timber is used to make strong triangulated trussed roof structures. These are designed to carry the weight of the roof with each member playing an important part, so any alteration may dangerously weaken the structure. If your house is relatively new you should check with the company that built it, or with a local builder, whether it is safe to proceed.

If you have a choice, site the hatchway over a landing, but not close to a stair, rather than in a room. In this way a ladder used for access will not interfere with the occupants or function of the room, and furniture arrangements are not affected. Allow for the pitch of the roof, as you will need headroom above the hatch.

Making the opening
If you are planning to fit a special folding loft ladder, the size of the new opening will be specified by the manufacturer. Generally aim to cut away no more than one of the ceiling joists: these are usually spaced 400mm (1ft 4in) apart.

Locate three of the joists by drilling or boring pilot holes in the ceiling. Mark out a square for the opening between the two outer joists. Cut an inspection hole inside the marked area to check with a mirror there are no obstacles in the way of the cutting line. Saw through the plasterwork and take it down.

Pass a light into the roof space and climb up into it between the joists. Lay a board across the joists to support yourself. Saw through the middle joist, cutting it back 50mm (2in) from each edge of the opening. Cut two new lengths of joist timber – called trimmers – to fit between the joists. Allow for a 12mm (½in) deep square housing at each end (1). Nail the housed joints and the butt joints between the trimmer joists. Use two 100mm (4in) round wire nails to secure each joist.

Nail the ceiling laths or plasterboard to the underside of the trimmer joists. Cut timber linings to cover the joists and the edges of the plaster. Make good the damaged edges of the plaster with filler. When set, nail mitred architrave moulding around the opening. Make a drop-in or hinged panel of 18mm (¾in) plywood or blockboard. If you plan to use the loft space mainly for storage, fix chipboard panels over the joists (▷). Cut them to fit through the opening.

SEE ALSO

Details for: ▷
Chipboard-flooring	54
Laying chipboard	57

Alternative ways to install hatch covers

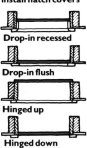

Drop-in recessed

Drop-in flush

Hinged up

Hinged down

Housing joints
A housing joint will give better support to the trimmer joist than nails alone.

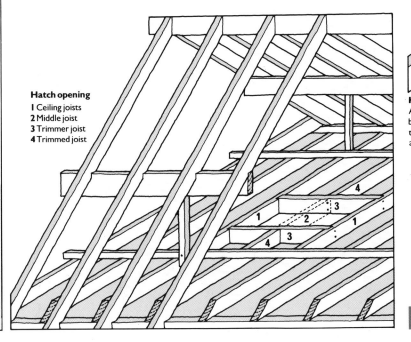

Hatch opening
1 Ceiling joists
2 Middle joist
3 Trimmer joist
4 Trimmed joist

33

INTERIOR PLASTERWORK

Plasterwork is used to provide internal walls and ceilings with a smooth, flat surface suitable for decorating with paint or paper. The plaster also provides sound and thermal insulation as well as protection from fire. Decorative mouldings – a feature of walls and ceilings in many older houses – are also made of plaster; they're still available for renovations. There are basically two methods for providing a plaster finish: the traditional way is wet plastering; the modern one uses plasterboard, and is known as 'dry lining'.

Traditional plastering techniques

Traditional plastering uses a mix of plastering materials and water, which is spread over the rough background in one, two or even three layers. Each layer is applied with a trowel and levelled accordingly; when set, the plaster forms an integral part of the wall or ceiling. The background may be solid masonry for walls, or timber-framed walls and ceilings finished with lath-and-plaster. Laths are thin strips of wood nailed to the timber framework to support plaster, which, forced between the laths, spreads to form nibs that grip on the other side. With traditional plastering, it takes practice to achieve a smooth, flat surface over a large area. With care, an amateur can produce satisfactory results, provided the right tools and plaster are employed and the work is divided into manageable sections. All-purpose one-coat plasters are now available to make traditional plastering easier for amateurs.

Dry lining with plasterboard

Manufactured boards of paper-covered plaster are widely used to dry-line the walls and ceilings in modern homes and during renovations. Its use overcomes the drying out period required for wet plasters and requires less skill to apply.

The large flat boards are nailed or bonded to walls and ceilings to provide a separate finishing layer. The surface may be decorated directly once the boards are sealed, or covered with a thin coat of finish plaster.

Storing plaster
Keep an open bag of plaster in a plastic sack sealed with adhesive tape.

Traditional Plastering
(Right)
The construction of a lath-and-plaster ceiling and plastered masonry wall.
1 Brick background
2 Ceiling joists
3 Lath background
4 Rendering coat
5 Floating coat
6 Finishing coat
7 Cornice moulding

Dry lining
(Far right)
The construction of a modern dry-lined wall and ceiling.
1 Block background
2 Batten fixing
3 Ceiling joists
4 Noggings
5 Plasterboard
6 Coving
7 Tape
8 Filler

BUYING AND STORING PLASTER

Plaster powder is normally sold in 50kg (1cwt) paper sacks. Smaller sizes, including 2.5kg (5½lb) bags are available from DIY stores for repair work. It's generally more economical to buy the larger sacks, but this depends on the scale of the work. Try to buy only as much plaster as you need. It's better to overestimate, however, to allow for wastage and prevent running short (◁).

Store plaster in dry conditions: if it is to be kept in an outbuilding for some time, cover it with plastic sheeting to protect it from moisture. Keep the paper bags off a concrete floor by placing them on boards or plastic sheeting. Open bags are more likely to absorb moisture, which can shorten the setting time and weaken the plaster. Keep an opened bag in a sealed plastic sack. Use self-adhesive tape to seal it. Discard plaster which contains lumps.

Ready-to-use plaster is also available in plastic tubs. It can be more expensive to buy it this way but it is easier for amateurs to use and it will keep for a long time, provided the airtight lid is well sealed.

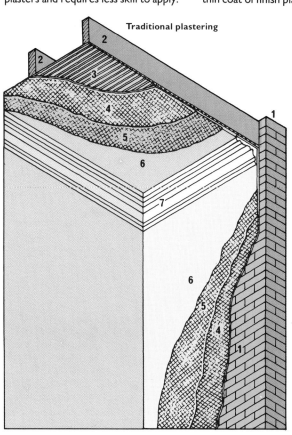

Traditional plastering

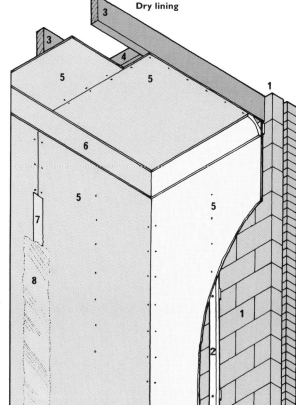

Dry lining

TYPES OF PLASTER

Plastering is carried out using modern gypsum plasters or mixes based on cement, lime and sand. By varying the process and introducing additives, a range of plasters can be produced within a given type to suit different background materials.

Plasters are basically produced in two grades – one as a base or 'floating' coat, the other for finishing coats. Base coat gypsum plasters are pre-mixed types, which contain lightweight aggregates. Base coat sanded plasters which are based on cement or cement/lime have to be mixed on site with a suitable grade of clean, sharp sand (although finish plasters are ready to use with the addition of water).

The following information deals only with those materials suitable for domestic work.

SEE ALSO

Details for: ▷
Applications   37

CHOOSING PLASTERS FOR DOMESTIC WORK

GYPSUM PLASTERS

Most plasters in common use are produced from ground gypsum rock by a process which removes most of the moisture from the rock to produce a powder that sets hard when mixed with water. Setting times are controlled by the use of retarding additives which give each of the several types of plaster a setting time suitable to its use.

Gypsum plasters are intended for interior work only, they should not be used on permanently damp walls. They must not be remixed with water once they start to set.

PLASTER OF PARIS

This quick-setting non-retarded gypsum plaster gives off heat as it sets. It is white or pinkish, and is mixed to a creamy consistency with clean water. It is unsuitable for general plastering but good for casting, and can be used for repairs to decorative mouldings.

CARLITE PLASTER

Carlite refers to a range of retarded gypsum plasters which are premixed with a lightweight aggregate and need only water to prepare them for use. The undercoat bonds well to most backgrounds, and this, coupled with their light weight – about half that of plasters mixed with sand – makes Carlite plasters fairly easy to use. The lightweight aggregate also gives improved thermal insulation. Setting time for Carlite plasters is about 1 to 2 hours.

Three types of Carlite undercoat plasters – 'browning', 'bonding' and 'metal lathing' – are available, each formulated to suit a background of a particular surface texture and suction. Browning is generally used for backgrounds with average suction, such as brickwork. For low-suction surfaces like dense brick and concrete blocks the bonding undercoat is preferred. The metal lathing is less commonly used and is primarily for metal lath backgrounds.

When more than one undercoat layer is needed to build up a thickness the same plaster should be used for all layers to ensure compatibility.

There is only one Carlite finishing plaster and it can be used over all the undercoats, being applied as soon as the undercoat has set.

THISTLE PLASTERS

Thistle is the brand name of a range of building plasters used for a variety of conditions and backgrounds.

Two types of finishing plaster are made, both mixed with water only: the finish plaster, for use over sanded undercoats, and the board finish plaster, used for finishing plasterboard surfaces.

Two special 'renovating' plasters are for use on walls with residual dampness. The undercoat is a pre-mixed gypsum plaster with special additives and the finish, formulated specially for use with the undercoat, contains a fungicide. The plaster is for use on damp walls which are slow to dry out, as in new, exposed building work or in old houses with new damp-proof courses installed. The plaster is not itself a damp-proofing material, but it allows the background material to breathe and dry out without letting the moisture show on the surface.

The cause of the problem must be dealt with before the plaster is applied.

SIRAPITE B

Sirapite B is a finish coat gypsum plaster for use over undercoats which contain sand, including cement rendering. It is not suitable for application to plasterboard. Only water is needed to prepare it. It contains additives which improve its workability, it has a gradual, progressive set and it can be brought to a high standard of finish.

Sirapite B is widely used by skilled professional plasterers.

SANDED PLASTERS

Before the advent of modern gypsums, lime and sand for undercoats and neat lime for finishes were used in traditional wet plastering, often with animal hair added to the undercoat mix as a binder. Lime plasters are generally less strong than gypsum and cement-based plasters.

Lime is still used, but mainly as an additive to improve the workability of a sand and cement plaster or rendering Cement-based sanded plaster undercoats may be required by some authorities for kitchen and bathroom walls constructed on timber and expanded-metal lathing. These undercoats can also be used on old brickwork or where a strong impact-resistant covering is required.

SINGLE-COAT PLASTERS

A universal one-coat plaster can, as its name implies, be used in a single application on a variety of backgrounds and trowelled to a normal finish.

The plaster is available in 40kg (88lb) bags and only water is added to prepare it for use. It will stay workable for up to an hour and can be built up to a thickness of 50mm (2in) in one coat.

One-coat plaster is also available in small packs contained in mixing tubs, and these are ideal for such small repair jobs as making good where a fireplace has been removed. For larger areas than this it is more economical to buy bigger bags and mix on a board in the usual way.

FILLERS

Fillers are fine plaster powders used for repairs. Some, reinforced with cellulose resin, are sold in small packs and need only mixing with clean water for use. They are non-shrinking, adhere well and are ideal for filling cracks and holes in plaster and wood. Extra-fine fillers are also available ready-mixed in small tubs for levelling dents in woodwork.

● **Avoiding old plaster**
Plaster may deteriorate if stored for more than two months so suppliers try to ensure it is sold in rotation. The paper sacks in which plaster is supplied are usually date-stamped by the manufacturer. If you are buying from a self-service supplier, choose a sack with the latest date.

TYPES OF SURFACE

● **Providing a 'key'**
Rake out mortar
joints to help plaster
and cement
renderings grip.

A well-prepared background is the first step to successful plastering. New surfaces of block or brickwork may need only dampening or priming with a bonding agent, depending on their absorbency. *Old plastered surfaces needing repair should be thoroughly checked. If the plaster has 'blown', hack it off back to sound material, then treat the surface and replaster the area.*

Background preparation and absorbency

Brush down the surface of a masonry background to remove loose particles, dust and efflorescent salts (◁). Test the absorption of the background by splashing on water; if it stays wet, consider the surface 'normal' – this means that it will only require light dampening with clean water prior to applying the plaster.

A dry background which absorbs the water immediately takes too much water from the plaster, making it difficult to work, prevents it from setting properly and can result in cracking. Soak the masonry with clean water applied with a brush.

High-absorbency surfaces

For very absorbent surfaces, such as aerated concrete blocks, prime the background with 1 part PVA bonding agent: 3 to 5 parts clean water. When dry, apply a bonding coat of 3 parts bonding agent: 1 part water. Apply the plaster when the bonding coat is tacky.

Low-absorbency surfaces

Prime low-absorption smooth brickwork or concrete with a solution of 1 part bonding agent: 3 to 5 parts water. Allow to dry. Apply a second coat of 3 to 5 parts bonding agent: 1 part water, and apply the plaster when tacky or allow it to dry for no more than 24 hours before plastering.

Non-absorbent surfaces

Glazed tiles and painted walls are considered non-absorbent and will require a coating of neat bonding agent to enable the plaster to stick. The plaster is applied while the agent is still wet. An alternative for glazed tiles is to apply a slurry of 2 parts sharp sand: 1 part cement mixed with a solution of 1 part bonding agent: 1 part water. Apply the slurry with a stiff-bristled brush to form a stippled coating. Allow to dry for 24 hours then apply the plaster.

Another option is to chip off the old tiles. Always remove loose tiles.

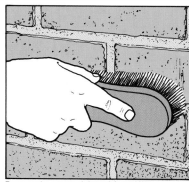
Remove loose particles with a stiff brush

Prime porous surfaces to control the suction

A bonding agent improves adhesion

Smooth tiles can be 'keyed' with a slurry

MAKING FILLER AND MORTAR BOARDS

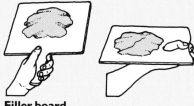

Filler board
You can make a useful board for mixing and working with filler from 6mm (¼in) marine plywood. Cut out a 300mm (1ft) square with a projecting handle on one side, or make a thumb hole like an artist's palette. Seal the surface with a polyurethane varnish or apply a plastic laminate for a smooth finish.

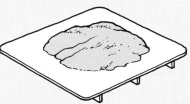

Mortar board
Cut a piece of 12mm (½in) or 18mm (¾in) marine plywood approximately 900mm (3ft) square. Round off the corners and chamfer the edges all round. Screw three lengths of 50 x 25mm (2 x 1in) softwood across the underside, spread equally apart. A smaller board, known as a 'spotboard', 600mm (2ft) square, can be made in a similar way.

Using a stand ▶
You will find it easier to handle plaster with the mix at table height.

Using a stand
A stand is used to support the mortar board at table height, about 700mm (2ft 4in) from the ground. This enables the plaster to be picked up on a hawk by placing it under the edge of the board and drawing the plaster onto it (◁).

Make a folding stand using 50 x 38mm (2 x 1½in) softwood for the legs and 75 x 25mm (3 x 1in) softwood for the rails. Make one leg frame fit inside the other and bolt them securely together at the centre.

A portable Workmate bench can be used to support the board instead of making a stand: grip the centre batten in the vice jaws.

MIXING PLASTER

With the background prepared, the next step for the amateur plasterer is to make a good mix. It is best to mix your plaster close to the working place, as it can be messy. Also cover the floor with old newspapers and remember to wipe your feet when leaving the room.

A plaster that is well mixed to the right consistency will be easier to apply. Use a plastic bucket to acccurately measure the cement, lime and sand, or plaster. For large quantities of plaster, multiply the number of bucket measures. For small quantities, just use half-bucket measures or less.

Old hard plaster stuck to your equipment can shorten the setting time and reduce the strength of the newly mixed plaster. Do not try to re-work plaster that has begun to set by adding more water: discard it and make a fresh batch. Mix only as much plaster as you will need. For larger areas, mix as much as you can apply in about twenty minutes – judge this by practice.

BONDING AGENTS

Bonding agents modify the suction of the background or improve the adhesion of the plastering. When used, the base coat plaster should not exceed 10mm (3/8in) in thickness. If you need to build up the thickness, scratch the surface to provide an extra key, and allow at least 24 hours between coats.

Bonding agents can be mixed with plaster or sand and cement to fill cracks. First brush away any loose particles and then apply a solution of 1 part agent: 3 to 5 parts water with a brush.

Mix the plaster or sand and cement with 1 part bonding agent: 3 parts water to a stiff mix. Apply the filler with a trowel pressing it well into the crack.

Wash tools and brushes thoroughly in clean water when you are finished. It may be necessary to rinse out the brushes as the work progresses on a large job.

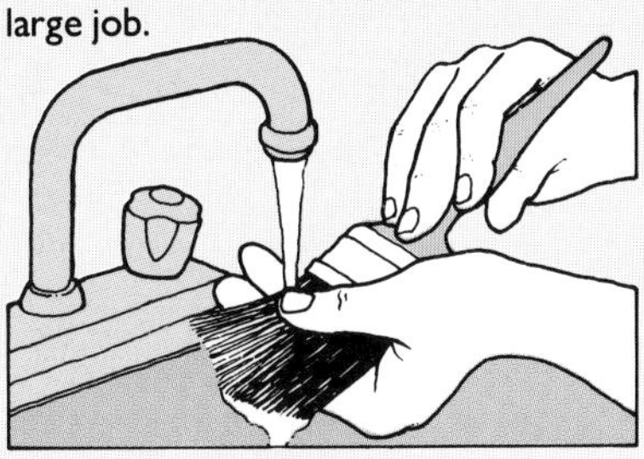

Wash agent from brushes before it sets

Base coat plasters

Mix base coat plasters on a mortar board (see opposite). For sanded plasters, measure out each of the materials and thoroughly dry-mix them with a shovel or trowel for small quantities (▷). Make a well in the heaped plaster and pour in some clean water. Turn in the plaster, adding water to produce a thick, creamy consistency.

Just add water to pre-mixed gypsum plaster (which already contains an aggregate). Mix them on the board in the same way. Always wash down the board after use.

You can mix small quantities of pre-mixed plaster in a bucket. Pour the plaster into the water and stir to a creamy consistency; 1kg (2lb 4oz) of plaster will need about 0.75 of a litre (1 1/3 pints) of water.

SEE ALSO

Details for: ▷
Builder's tools 76

Finish plaster

Mix finish plaster in a clean plastic bucket. Add the powder to the water. Pour not more than 2 litres (4 pints) of water into the bucket. Sprinkle the plaster into the water and stir it with a stout length of wood to a thick, creamy consistency. Tip the plaster out onto a clean, damp mortar board ready for use. Wash the bucket out with clean water before the plaster sets in it.

PLASTER TYPES, APPLICATION AND COVERAGE.

Type	Background	Type of coat	Coat thickness	Average ● coverage
CARLITE				
Browning *Normal suction*	Brick walls	Undercoat	10mm (3/8in)	6.5-7.5 sq.m. (7 3/4-9 sq yd)
	Block walls	Undercoat	10mm (3/8in)	6.5-7.5 sq.m. (7 3/4-9 sq yd)
	Concrete bricks	Undercoat	10mm (3/8in)	6.5-7.5 sq.m. (7 3/4-9 sq yd)
	Coarse concrete	Undercoat	10mm (3/8in)	6.5-7.5 sq.m. (7 3/4-9 sq yd)
Bonding *Low suction*	Brick walls	Undercoat	10mm (3/8in)	5.0-8.25 sq.m. (6-9 3/4 sq yd)
	Block walls	Undercoat	10mm (3/8in)	5.0-8.25 sq.m. (6-9 3/4 sq yd)
	Concrete bricks	Undercoat	10mm (3/8in)	5.0-8.25 sq.m. (6-9 3/4 sq yd)
	Smooth pre-cast concrete	Undercoat	8mm (5/16in)	5.0-8.25 sq.m. (6-9 3/4 sq yd)
	Plasterboards (Greyface)	Undercoat	8mm (5/16in)	5.0-8.25 sq.m. (6-9 3/4 sq yd)
	Polystyrene	Undercoat	10mm (3/8in)	5.0-8.25 sq.m. (6-9 3/4 sq yd)
Metal lathing	Expanded metal	Undercoat	10mm (3/8in)	3.0-3.5 sq.m. (3 1/2-4 sq yd)
Finish	Carlite plaster Undercoats	Finish top coat	2mm (1/16in)	20.5-25.0 sq.m. (24 1/2-30 sq yd)
THISTLE				
Finish	Sanded undercoats	Finish top coat	2mm (1/16in)	17.5-22.5 sq.m. (21-27 sq yd)
Board Finish	Plasterboards (Greyface)	Finish top coat	5mm (3/16in)	8.0-8.5 sq.m. (9 1/2-10 sq yd)
Renovating *Normal suction*	Brick walls	Undercoat	10mm (3/8in)	6.0 sq.m. (7 sq yd)
	Block walls	Undercoat	10mm (3/8in)	6.0 sq.m. (7 sq yd)
	Concrete bricks	Undercoat	10mm (3/8in)	6.0 sq.m. (7 sq yd)
Renovating finish	Renovating plaster	Finish top coat	2mm (1/16in)	19.0-21.0 sq.m. (22 3/4-25 sq yd)
SIRAPITE				
	Sanded undercoats	Finish top coat	3mm (1/8in)	12.5-13.5 sq.m. (15-16 sq yd)
ONE COAT				
	All types	Undercoat/finish	12mm (1/2in)	4.5 sq.m. (5 1/2 sq yd)

● m^2 per 50kg (sq yd per 50kg)

Plaster fillers

Pour out a small heap of the powder on to a small board, make a hollow in its centre and pour in water. Stir the mix to a creamy thickness; if it seems too runny add more powder. Use a rather drier mix for filling deeper holes.

APPLYING PLASTER

To the beginner plastering can seem a daunting business, yet it has only two basic requirements: that the plaster should stick well to its background and that it should be brought to a smooth, flat finish. Good preparation, the careful choice of plaster and working with the right tools should ensure good adhesion of the material, but the ability to achieve the smooth, flat surface will come only after some practice. Most of the plasterer's tools (◁) are rather specialized and unlikely to be found in the ordinary jobbing toolkit, but their cost may prove economical in the long term if you are planning several jobs.

Problems to avoid

Uneven surfaces
Many amateurs tackle plastering jobs, large or small, planning to rub the surface down level when it has set. This approach is very dust-creating and laborious, and invariably produces a poor result. If a power sander is used the dust is unpleasant to work in and permeates other parts of the house, making more work. Far better to try for a good surface as you put the plaster on, using wide-bladed tools to spread the material evenly. Ridges left by the corners of trowel or knife can be carefully shaved down afterwards with the knife – not with abrasive paper.

When covering a large area with finishing plaster it is not always easy to see if the surface is flat as well as smooth. Look obliquely across the wall or shine a light across it from one side to detect any irregularities.

Crazing
Fine cracks in finished plaster may be due to a sand-and-cement undercoat still drying out, and therefore shrinking. Such an undercoat must be fully dry before the plaster goes on, though if the plaster surface is sound the fine cracks can be wallpapered over.

Top coat and undercoat plaster can also crack if made to dry out too fast. Never heat plaster to dry it out.

Loss of strength
Gypsum and cement set chemically when mixed with water. If they dry out before the chemical set takes place they do not develop their full strength, and become friable. Should this happen it may be necessary to strip the wall and replaster it.

PLASTERING TECHNIQUES

Picking up
Hold the edge of the hawk below the mortar board and scrape a manageable amount of plaster onto the hawk, using the trowel **(1)**. Take no more than a trowelful to start with.

Tip the hawk towards you and in one movement cut away about half of the plaster with the trowel, scraping and lifting it off the hawk and onto the face of the trowel **(2)**.

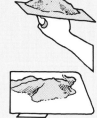

1 Load the hawk   **2 Lift off the plaster**

Application
Hold the loaded trowel horizontally but tilted at an angle to the face of the wall **(1)**. Apply the plaster with a vertical upward stroke, pressing firmly so that plaster is fed to the wall. Flatten the angle of the trowel as you go **(2)** but never let its whole face come into contact with the plaster as suction can pull it off the wall again.

1 Tilt the trowel   **2 Apply the plaster**

Levelling up
Build a slight extra thickness of plaster with the trowel, applying it as evenly as possible. Use the rule (◁) to level the surface, starting at the bottom of the wall, the rule held against original plaster or wooden screeds nailed on at either side. Work the rule upwards while moving it from side to side, then lift it carefully away and the surplus plaster with it. Fill in any hollows with more plaster from the trowel, then level again. Let the plaster stiffen before a final smoothing with the trowel.

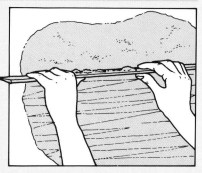

Work the rule up the wall to level the surface

Finishing
You can apply the finishing coat to a gypsum plaster undercoat as soon as it is set. A cement-based sanded plaster must dry thoroughly, but dampen its surface to adjust suction before finish-plastering. The grey face of plasterboard is finished immediately and is not wetted.

Apply the finish with a plasterer's trowel as described above, spreading it evenly, no more than 2 to 3mm (1/16 to 1/8in) judging this by eye, as screeds are not used. To plasterboard apply two coats to build a 5mm (3/16in) thickness.

As the plaster stiffens, brush or lightly spray it with water, then trowel the surface to consolidate it and produce a smooth matt finish. Avoid pressing hard and overworking the surface. Lastly remove surplus water with a sponge.

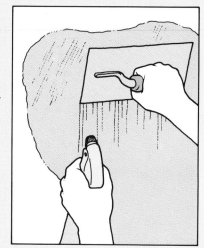

Spray plaster occasionally as you smooth it

PLASTERING A WALL

The plastering of a complete wall is not likely to be required in many households. Any new work is much more easily carried out with plasterboard (▷), but there are times when repairs arising out of damp problems, or alterations such as moving doorways, *will leave large areas to be plastered, and this can be done by the non-professional. The key to success is to divide the wall into manageable areas (See below) though some previous practice, for example when patching up decayed plaster, would be of help.*

Applying the plaster

Using the face of the plasterer's trowel, scrape a couple of trowel-loads of plaster onto the hawk and start undercoat plastering at the top of the wall, holding the trowel at an angle to the face of the wall and applying the plaster with vertical strokes. Work from right to left if you are right handed and from left to right if you are left handed (See below).

Using firm pressure to ensure good adhesion, apply a first thin layer and then follow this with more plaster, building up the required thickness. If the final thickness of the plaster needs to be more than 10mm (⅜in), key the surface with a scratcher and let it set, then apply a second or 'floating' coat.

Fill in the area between two screed battens. It is not necessary to work tight up against them. Level the surface by running the rule upwards, laid across the battens, and working it from side to side as you go. Fill in any hollows and then level the plaster again. Scratch the surface lightly to provide a key for the finishing coat and let the plaster set. Work along the wall in this way, then remove the battens, and fill the gaps they have left between the plastered areas, again levelling with the rule.

With gypsum plasters the finishing coat can be applied as soon as the undercoat is set. Cement undercoats must be left to dry for at least 24 hours because of shrinkage, then wetted when the top coat is applied.

PREPARING TO PLASTER

In addition to the plastering tools you need a spirit level and some lengths of 10mm (⅜in) thick planed softwood battening. The battens – known as screeds – are for nailing to the wall to act as guides when it comes to levelling the plaster. Professional plasterers form 'plaster screeds' by applying bands of undercoat plaster to the required thickness. These may be vertical or horizontal.

Prepare the background (▷) and fix the wooden screeds vertically to the wall with masonry nails. Driving the nails fully home will make it easier for you to work the trowel, but it can also make it more difficult to remove the screeds afterwards. The screeds should be spaced no more than 600mm (2ft) apart. Use the spirit level to get them truly plumb, packing them out with strips of hardboard or wood as necessary.

Mix the undercoat plaster to a thick, creamy consistency and measure out two bucketfuls to begin with, though you can increase this to larger amounts when you become a little more proficient at working with the material.

Finishing

Cover the undercoat with a thin layer of finishing plaster, working from top to bottom and from left to right (See left) using even, vertical strokes. Work with the trowel held at a slight angle so that only its one edge is touching.

Make sweeping horizontal strokes to level the surface further. You can try using the rule in getting the initial surface even, but you may risk dragging the finish coat off. Use the trowel to smooth out any slight ripples.

Wet the trowel and work over the surface with firm pressure to consolidate the plaster, and as it sets trowel it to produce a smooth matt finish. Don't over work it, and wipe away any plaster slurry which appears with a damp sponge.

The wall should be left to dry out for some weeks before decorating.

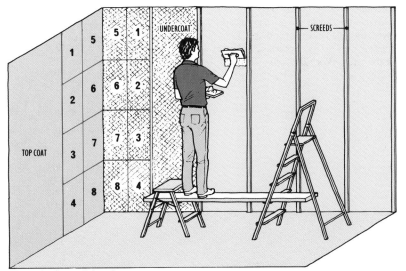

The order for applying plaster

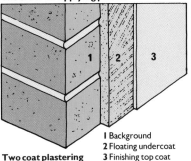

Two coat plastering

1 Background
2 Floating undercoat
3 Finishing top coat

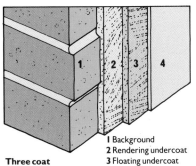

Three coat plastering

1 Background
2 Rendering undercoat
3 Floating undercoat
4 Finishing top coat

◄ Plaster layers
Plaster is applied in layers to build up a smooth level surface. Two or three coats may be used.

Plumb the screeds
Pack out the screed battens at the fixing points as required.

PLASTERBOARD

Plasterboard provides a relatively quick and simple method of smooth-covering the rough structural materials of walls and ceilings. It is easy to cut and to fix in place, either by bonding or nailing.

A range of dry-lining plasterboards is available from builders' merchants. The boards are all based on a core of aerated gypsum plaster covered on both sides with a strong paper liner. They may have a grey paper facing for finishing with plaster or an ivory-coloured paper for direct decorating with wallpaper or paint. As well as coming in a range of thicknesses and sheet sizes the boards can also have tapered or bevelled edges on the ivory-coloured sides (See below), though boards with square edges are used for most work. The edge on the grey side is always square.

Plasterboard provides good sound insulation and fire protection.

STORING AND CUTTING PLASTERBOARD

Plasterboard is fragile, having very little structural strength, and the sheets are quite heavy, so always get someone to help you carry a sheet, and hold it on its edge. To carry it flat is to run a serious risk of breaking it.

Manufacturers and suppliers of the material store it flat in stacks, but this is usually inconvenient at home and is anyway not necessary for a small number of sheets. Instead store them on edge, leaning them slightly against a wall, their ivory-coloured faces together to protect them.

Place the sheets down carefully to avoid damaging their edges.

Cutting plasterboard
Plasterboard can be cut with a saw or with a stiff-bladed craft knife.

The sheet must be supported, face side up, on lengths of wood laid across trestles and the cutting line marked on it with the aid of a straightedge. When sawing, the saw should be held at a shallow angle to the surface of the plasterboard, and if the off-cut is a large one an assistant should support it to prevent it breaking away towards the end of the cut.

When cutting plasterboard with a knife, cut well into the material following a straight edge, snap the board along the cutting line over a length of wood and cut through the paper liner on the other side to separate the pieces.

To make openings in plasterboard for electrical and other fittings you can use a keyhole saw, a power jigsaw or a sharp craft knife.

Remove any ragged paper after the cutting by rubbing down the cut edges with an abrasive paper.

Tapered edge

Square edge

Bevelled edge

Types of edge
Tapered and square-edged boards are most common and the joints of both are filled flush. Bevelled-edge boards are used for walls where the joints are featured.

PLASTERBOARD SPECIFICATIONS

PLASTERBOARD: TYPES, USAGE	WIDTHS	LENGTHS	THICKNESS	EDGE FINISH
Standard plasterboard				
This material is generally used for the dry lining of walls and ceilings. It is produced in as many as nine lengths, and though most suppliers stock only a limited range other sizes can be ordered. One side is ivory-coloured for direct decoration and the other is grey for plastering.	600mm (2ft) 900mm (3ft) 1.2m (4ft)	1.8m (6ft) to 3.6m (12ft) *Commonly stocked in 2.43m (8ft) and 3.0m (10ft) lengths*	9.5mm (⅜in) 12.7mm (½in) 12.7mm (½in)	Tapered or square Bevelled
Baseboard				
Baseboard is a square-edged plasterboard that is lined with grey paper and is produced as a backing for a plaster finish. It is used mainly for plastered ceilings.	914mm (3ft)	1.2m (4ft) 1.22m (4ft) 1.35m (4ft 5in) 1.37m (4ft 6in)	9.5mm (⅜in)	Square
Lath board				
Lath board is used similarly to baseboard but has its long edges rounded.	406mm (1ft 4in)	1.2m (4ft) 1.22m (4ft) 1.35m (4ft 5in) 1.37m (4ft 6in)	9.5mm (⅜in) 12.7mm (½in)	Round
Thermal insulation board				
Thermal insulation boards are standard sheets of plasterboard with a backing of expanded polystyrene or urethane laminate. The paper surface may be ivory-coloured for direct decoration or grey for plastering.	1.2m (4ft)	2.4m (7ft 10½in) 2.43m (8ft) 2.7m (8ft 10¼in)	25mm (1in) 32mm (1¼in) 40mm (1⅝in) 50mm (2in) *thickness only available for polystyrene backed*	Tapered or square
Vapour-check plasterboard				
These boards have a tough metallized polyester film backing which is vapour resistant and provides reflective thermal insulation. They are used as an internal lining to prevent warm moist air condensing on or inside structural wall or ceiling materials.	406mm (1ft 4in) 900mm (3ft) 914mm (3ft) 1.2m (4ft)	*Stocked in same lengths as standard board, baseboard, and lath*	*Stocked in same thicknesses as standard board, baseboard and lath*	Tapered, square or round

N.B. Metric sizes actual, imperial size approximate

PLASTERBOARDING A WALL

Plasterboard can be nailed directly on to the timber framework of a stud partition or on to wooden battens that are fixed to a solid masonry wall. It can also be bonded straight onto solid walls with plaster or an adhesive.

The boards may be fitted horizontally if it is more economical to do so, but generally they are placed vertically. All of the edges should be supported.

When plasterboarding a ceiling and walls, cover the ceiling first.

Methods of fixing plasterboard

Nailing to a stud partition
Timber-framed partition walls may be simply plain room-dividers or they may include doorways. When you are plasterboarding a plain wall you should work from one corner when you start fixing the boards, but where there is a doorway you should work away from it towards the corners.

Starting from a corner
Using the footlifter, try the first board in position. Mark and scribe the edge that meets the adjacent wall if this is necessary (▷), then nail the board into position, securing it to all the frame members (See right).

Fix the rest of the boards in place, working across the partition. Butt the edges of tapered-edged boards, but leave a gap of 3mm (⅛in) between boards that are going to be coated with a board-finishing plaster.

If necessary, scribe the edge of the last board to fit the end corner before nailing it into place.

Cut a skirting board, mitring the joints at the corners or scribing the ends of the new board to the original (▷). Fit the skirting board.

Starting from a doorway
Using the footlifter, position the first board flush with the door stud and mark the position of the underside of the door's head member on the edge of the board. Between the mark on the board's edge and its top edge cut out a strip 25mm (1in) wide. Reposition the board and fix it in place, nailing it to all frame members (See right).

Fix the rest of the boards in place, working towards the corner. Butt the edges of tapered-edge boards but leave a 3mm (⅛in) gap all round boards which are to be coated afterwards with a board-finishing plaster.

If necessary, scribe the last board to fit any irregularities in the corner (▷) before fixing it in place.

Cover the rest of the wall on the other side of the doorway in the same way, starting by cutting a 25mm (1in) strip from the first board between its top edge and a mark indicating the lower side of the door's head member.

Cut a plasterboard panel to go above the doorway, butting into the cutouts in the boards on each side of the door. Sandpaper away the ragged edges of paper before fitting the panel.

When all of the plasterboard is in place fill and finish the joints (▷). Cut and fit door linings (▷) and cover the edges with an architrave moulding.

Cut and fit skirtings (▷), nailing through the plasterboard into alternate studs underneath.

NAIL FIXING

Use special galvanized plasterboard nails of lengths appropriate to the thickness of the plasterboard, as shown in the table below.

Space the nails 150mm (6in) apart and place them not less than 10mm (⅜in) from the paper-covered edge and 12mm (½in) from the cut ends. Drive the nails in straight so that they sink just below the surface without tearing through the paper lining.

Board thickness	Nail length
9.5mm (⅜in)	32mm (1¼in)
12.7mm (½in)	40mm (1⅝in)
19mm (¾in)	50mm (2in)
25mm (1in)	50mm (2in)
32mm (1¼in)	63mm (2½in)
40mm (1⅝in)	63mm (2½in)
50mm (2in)	75mm (3in)

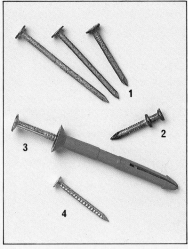

Plasterboard nails
1 Galvanized nails
2 Double-headed nail
3 Nailable plug
4 Jagged nail

Types of nail used with plasterboard

●**Distances between stud centres**
When providing new supports it is cheaper to use 12.7mm (½in) thick board on studs set 600mm (2ft) apart. Maximum distance between stud centres: for 9.5mm (⅜in) board – 450mm (1ft 6in), for 12.7mm to 50mm (½ to 2in) thick board – 600mm (2ft).

Using a footlifter
Cut the board about 16mm (⅝in) below room height to clear the footlifter, a simple tool that holds the board against the ceiling leaving both hands free for nailing. You can make one from a 75mm (3in) wide wood block.

Order for plasterboarding
Plasterboarding sequence. Work away from a corner for a plain wall, otherwise work away from a doorway.

SCRIBING PLASTERBOARD

If the inner edge of the first sheet of plasterboard butts against an uneven wall, or its other edge does not fall on the centre of the stud, the board must be scribed to fit.

Scribing the first board

Try the first board in position (1). The case shown is of an uneven wall pushing the plasterboard beyond the stud at the other edge of the plasterboard, and of the problem encountered when the end stud in a partition is not set at the normal spacing.

Move and reposition the board (2) so that its inner edge lies on the centre of the stud and tack it into place with plasterboard nails driven part way into the intermediate studs. Before temporarily fixing the board make sure it is set at the right height by using the foot lifter. With a pencil and a batten (cut to the width of the board) trace a line down the face of the board, echoing the contour of the wall. It is essential to keep the batten level while doing this.

Trim the waste away from the scribed edge, following the line, replace the board in the corner and fix it with plasterboard nails (3).

Scribing the last board

Temporarily nail the board to be scribed over the last fixed board (4), ensuring that their edges lie flush.

Using a batten and a pencil as above, trace a pencil line down the face of the board, using the batten as a guide and carefully keeping it level.

Remove the marked board, cut away the scribed area to cut it to size and nail it into place (5).

1 Try the first board in the corner

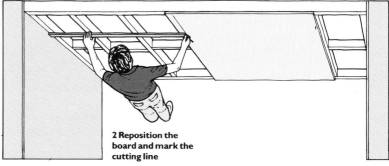

2 Reposition the board and mark the cutting line

3 Cut the board to size and nail in place

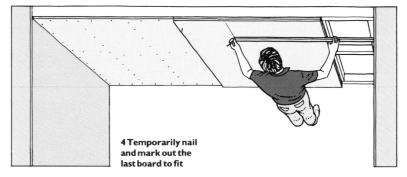

4 Temporarily nail and mark out the last board to fit

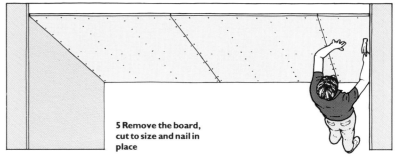

5 Remove the board, cut to size and nail in place

SOLID WALL FURRING

Plasterboard cannot be nailed directly to solid masonry walls. Battens of sawn timber known as furring strips are used to provide a good fixing for the nails and to counter any unevenness of the wall surface. These should be treated with a wood preservative.

You can cover sound old plaster but if it is in poor condition strip it back to the brickwork. If the failure of the original plaster was caused by damp, it must be treated and if possible allowed to dry out before lining.

Fit any plumbing pipe runs, electrical conduit or cable to the wall before the battens are fixed to conceal them.

Marking out

Use a straightedge to mark the position of the strips on the wall with vertical chalk lines. The lines should be placed at 400mm (1ft 4in), 450mm (1ft 6in) or 600mm (2ft) centres according to the width and thickness of the plasterboard being used, bearing in mind that sheets of plasterboard must meet on the centre lines of the battens. Work away from any door or window opening and allow for the thickness of the battens and plasterboard at the reveals (▷).

Fixing the battens

Cut the required number of furring battens from 50 x 25mm (2 x 1in) sawn softwood. The vertical battens should be cut 155mm (6¼in) less than the height of the wall. The horizontal battens should be cut to run along the tops and bottoms of the vertical ones and any short vertical infill battens above and below openings (See below).

Nail the vertical furring battens on first, setting their bottom ends 100mm (4in) above the floor. Fix them with masonry nails or cut nails, with the face of each batten level with the guide line (See right), and check with the straightedge and spirit level that they are also flat and plumb, packing them out if and as necessary.

Now nail the horizontal battens across the tops and bottoms of the vertical members, packing them to the same level if necessary.

Fixing the plasterboard

To fix plasterboard to furring strips follow the same procedure as described for nailing to a stud partition (▷), except that in this case the boards at the sides of doors and windows do not need to be notched to receive panels above or below the openings.

The procedure for filling and finishing the joints between the sheets of plasterboard is also identical.

Cut the skirting board to length and nail it through the plasterboard to the bottom horizontal furring strip, though if it is a high skirting of the type used in old high-ceilinged houses it can be nailed to the vertical battens.

LEVELLING THE FURRING BATTENS

Masonry walls are often uneven and this must be taken into account when fixing the battens if the lining is to finish straight and flat.

To check if the wall is flat hold a long straightedge horizontally against it at different levels. If it proves to be uneven, mark the vertical chalk line already drawn on the wall which is the closest to the highest point (**1**).

Hold a straight furring batten vertically on the marked chalk line keeping it plumb with a straightedge and spirit level, then mark the floor (**2**) where the face of the batten falls. Draw a straight guide line across the floor (**3**), passing through this mark and meeting the walls on each end at right angles.

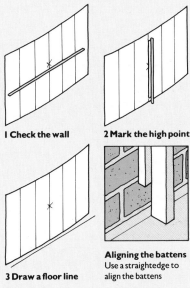

1 Check the wall

2 Mark the high point

3 Draw a floor line

Aligning the battens
Use a straightedge to align the battens

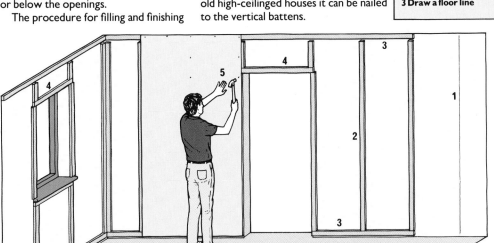

Using furring strips
Order of working
1 Mark batten positions
2 Fix vertical battens
3 Fix horizontal battens
4 Fix short pieces over doors and windows and offset the short vertical ones.
5 Nail boards in place working away from a door or window

43

BONDING TO A SOLID WALL

As an alternative to using batten fixing for dry-lining a solid wall, tapered-edged plasterboard can be bonded directly to the wall with dabs of plaster or an adhesive. Special pads are produced for levelling up the wall, but squares cut from remnants of the plasterboard itself can be used.

The pads are first bonded to the wall in lines that substitute for battens, then dabs of plaster are applied between the lines of pads and the plasterboard is temporarily nailed to the pads while the plaster sets. The special double-headed nails are then removed.

Boards 900mm (3ft) wide are usually used with this technique. The wall must first be prepared in the usual way (◁).

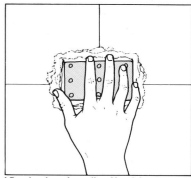

I Bond pads to the wall and level them

Fixing the pads

Set out vertical chalk lines on the wall 450mm (1ft 6in) apart, working from one corner or from a doorway or window opening (See below).

Draw a horizontal line 225mm (9in) from the ceiling, one 100mm (4in) from the floor and another centred between them. If the wall is more than 2.4m (8ft) high divide the space between the top and bottom equally with two lines. The pads are placed where the horizontal and vertical lines intersect.

Using a spirit level and a straightedge almost the height of the wall, check the wall at each vertical line, noting high spots at the intersections of the lines.

Bond a pad on the most prominent intersection point, using a bonding-coat plaster or a proprietary plaster adhesive, and press it in place to leave not less than 3mm (⅛in) of adhesive behind it (**I**). All the rest of the pads are levelled up to this first one with plaster or adhesive.

Bond and plumb the other pads on the same vertical line, then complete a second vertical row two lines from the first. Check these pads for level vertically, then diagonally with the first row. Work across the wall in this way, then fix the remaining pads on the other intersections. Allow two hours to set.

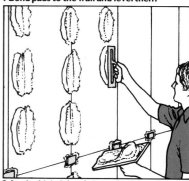

2 Apply thick dabs of plaster between the pads

Fixing the plasterboard

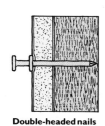

Double-headed nails
Use these special nails to temporarily hold the board while the plaster adhesive sets.

Apply thick dabs of adhesive or bonding plaster to the wall with a trowel (**2**) over an area for one board at a time. Space them 75mm (3in) apart vertically and do not overlap the area of the next board. Press the board firmly against the pads so that the plaster spreads out behind it. Use the straightedge to press it evenly and the footlifter to position it.

Check the alignment, then fix the board with double-headed nails driven through it into the pads round the edge. Fix the next board in the same way, butting it to the first, and work on across the wall, scribing the last board into the internal angle (◁). When the plaster has set remove the nails with pincers or a claw hammer, protecting the plasterboard surface (**3**).

Work round angles and openings (See opposite) and when all surfaces are covered fill and finish the joints (◁).

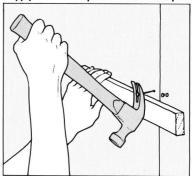

3 Pull out the nails when plaster is set

The bonding method order of working
I Mark pad positions
2 Stick the pads to the wall
3 Apply dabs of plaster
4 Place plasterboard and temporarily nail. Remove nails when plaster is set

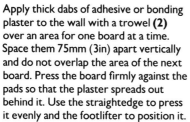

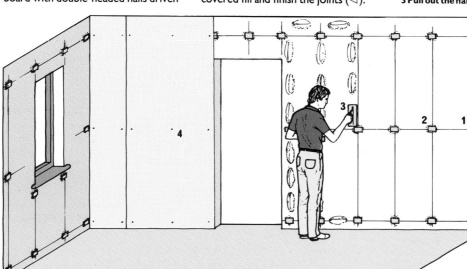

WINDOW OPENINGS

Cut the plasterboard linings for the window reveals and soffit to length and width. These are put into place before the wall linings. Their front edges should line up with the faces of the wall pads or furring strips.

Apply evenly spaced dabs of plaster adhesive to the back of the soffit lining, press it into place (1) and prop it there while the plaster adhesive sets. If the lining covers a wide span also use a wooden board to support it. Fit the reveal linings in the same way (2).

Working away from the window, fix the wall linings so that the paper-covered edge of the board laps the cut edge of the reveal lining.

The panels for above and below the window are cut and fitted last. Sandpaper off any rough edges of paper and leave a 3mm (⅛in) gap for filling.

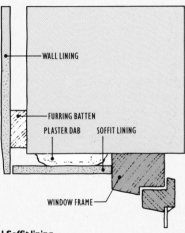

1 Soffit lining
Fix a soffit lining with dabs of plaster and prop in place until set

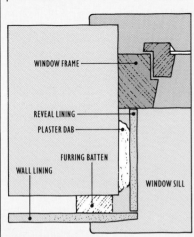

2 Reveal lining
Like the soffit lining, cut and fix the reveal so the wall lining overlaps its cut edge.

ANGLES AND OPENINGS

Internal angle

Fix wooden furring battens or bonded fibreboard pads close to the corner. Whenever possible always place the cut edges of the plasterboard into an internal corner.

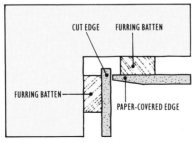

Internal corner
Set cut edges into the angle

External angle

Attach furring battens or fibreboard pads as close to the corner as possible. Use screws and wall plugs to fix the battens so as to prevent the corner breaking away. At least one board should have a paper-covered edge, which should lap the other.

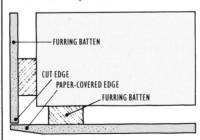

External corner
A paper-covered edge should lap the other edge

Door openings

The reveals of doorways in exterior walls should be treated in the same way as is described for window openings (See left).

In the case of interior door openings screw-fix timber furring strips or bond fibreboard pads level with the edge of the blockwork, then nail or bond the plasterboard wall linings into place.

Fit a new door lining or modify the old one if necessary and cover the joint with an architrave moulding.

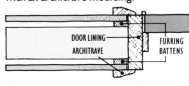

Electrical outlets

Depending on the type of fitting, chase the wall or pack out the mounting box for an electrical switch or socket outlet so that it finishes flush with the face of the plasterboard lining. Screw-fix short lengths of furring batten at each side of the box, or apply dabs of adhesive or plaster for pads if using the bonding method (See opposite).

Cut the opening for the box before fixing the board. If you find it difficult to mark the opening accurately by transferring measurements to the board, remove the fitting from the box and take an impression of it by placing the board in position and pressing it against the box.

Fix the plasterboard panel in place and replace the electrical fitting.

Interior door opening
Fit a new lining or widen the old one and cover the joint between the lining and plasterboard with an architrave.

Electrical outlets
Chase the wall or pack out the mounting box to set it flush with the plasterboard.

Angle treatments
Order of working
1 Fit soffit lining
2 Fit reveal lining
3 Fit boarding working away from window
4 Fit panels over and under window
5 Fit boarding working away from doorway
6 Cut and fit panel over doorway
7 Cut openings for electrical fittings as they occur

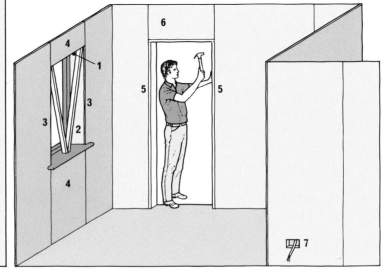

FINISHING PLASTERBOARD

All of the joints between boards and the indentations left by nailing must be filled and smoothed before the ivory-coloured surface of the *plasterboard is ready for direct decoration. You will need filler, finish and jointing tape.*

SEE ALSO

◁ Details for:
Metal beading   47

Tools and materials

The filler and finish are prepared for use by being mixed with water. The paper jointing tape is 53mm (2⅛in) wide with feathered edges, and is creased along its centre. It is used for reinforcing flat joints and internal angles. A special paper jointing tape is available for covering and reinforcing external angles. This tape has thin metal strips on each side of its central crease which strengthens the corners.

Skilled plasterers use purpose-made tools for finishing joints, but you can use medium and wide filling knives, a plaster's trowel and a close-textured plastic sponge.

Covering nails

Fill the indentations left by the nailing, using a filling knife to apply the filler and smooth it out.

When the filler has set apply a thin coating of finish and feather it off with a damp sponge.

Filling tapered-edge board joints

Mix the joint filler to a creamy consistency and apply a continuous band of it about 60mm (2½in) wide down the length of the joint.

Press the paper tape into the filler, using the medium size filling knife, bedding it in well and excluding air bubbles (**1**). Follow this with another layer of filler applied over the tape to level the surface, this time using the wide filling knife. When the filler has stiffened slightly, smooth its edges with the damp sponge, then let it set completely before filling any remaining small hollows.

When all the filler has set coat it with a thin layer of the joint finish. Mix the finish thoroughly to the consistency of thick cream and apply it in a wide band down the joint with a plasterer's trowel (**2**). Before it sets feather off its edges with the dampened sponge, and after it has set apply another thin but wider band over it, again feathering the edges with the sponge, working in a circular motion (**3**).

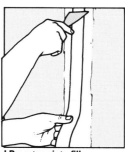

1 Press tape into filler

2 Apply finish in a wide band

3 Feather edge with a sponge

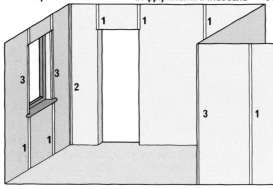

Filling the joints
1 Use the tape flat for flush jointing
2 Fold the tape for internal corners
3 Use metal-reinforced tape or metal beading on external corners (◁).

CUT EDGES

Treat a butt joint between a tapered edge and a cut edge of plasterboard in a way similar to that described for joints between two tapered edges (See left), but build up the tapered edge with filler, level with the cut edge, before applying the tape.

When two cut edges meet press the filler into the 3mm (⅛in) gap to finish flush. When the filler is set apply a thin band of finish to it and press the paper tape tight against the board. Cover this with a wide but thin coat of finish and feather the edges, then finish off as before.

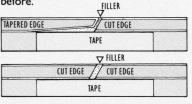

GLASS–FIBRE TAPE

A self-adhesive glass–fibre mesh tape can be used instead of traditional paper tape for jointing new plasterboard or for making patch repairs. The 50mm (2in) wide tape is a strong binder and does not need prior application of filler to bond it in place. The tape is put on first, then the filler is pressed through the mesh afterwards.

Applying the tape
Ensure that the jointing edges of the plasterboard are dust-free. If the edges of boards have been cut, burnish them with the handle of your filling knife to remove all traces of rough paper.

Starting at the top, centre the tape over the joint, unroll and press it into place as your work down the wall. Cut it off to length at the bottom. Do not overlap ends if you have to make a join in the tape; butt them.

Mix the filler and press it through the tape into the joint with the filling knife, then level off the surface so that the mesh of the tape is visible and let the filler set.

Finish the joint with finishing compound, as with paper tape.

Applying the filler
Press the filler through the tape with a filling knife.

FINISHING PLASTERBOARD

Internal corners

The internal corners of dry-lined walls are finished in a way similar to the method used for flat joints. Any gaps are first filled flush with filler and if necessary a band of PVA bonding agent is applied to the original ceiling or wall plaster to reduce its suction.

Cut the paper tape to length and fold it down its centre. Brush a thin band of finish on to each side of the corner and press the paper into it while it is wet. You can use a square section length of wood to press down both sides at once to remove air bubbles (1).

With a filling knife apply a 75mm (3in) wide band of finish to both sides of the corner immediately and feather the edges with a damp sponge (2).

When the finish is set apply a second, wider coat and feather the edges again.

1 Press into the corner with a wooden block   **2 Apply a wide band of finish and feather edge**

External corners

When finishing an external corner joint of plasterboard use the metal-reinforced corner tape. Cut it to length, fold it down its centre, apply a 50mm (2in) wide band of filler down both sides of the corner and bond the tape on it using a wide filling knife to keep the corner straight. Press the tape down well so that the metal strips are bedded firmly against the plasterboard, except when tapered edged board is used and the corner tape is filled out flush with the surface. Apply two coats of finish, feathering the edges as for internal corners (1).

For a very vulnerable corner use a length of metal angle bead. Apply a coating of filler to each side of the corner, then bed the angle bead in it, flushing it off with a knife before leaving it to set (2).

Apply a second coat of filler to both sides in a wide band and feather it off with a damp sponge.

When the filler is set apply two coats of finish, feathering off as before.

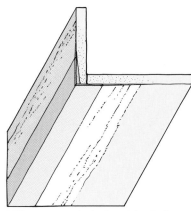

1 Fill out a tapered-edge board then bed tape

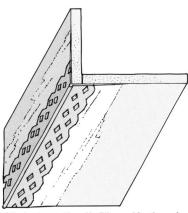

2 Embed metal bead in filler and feather edge

PREPARING FOR DECORATION

Finishing with plaster

The alternative to direct decoration of the ivory-coloured side of plasterboard is to precede decoration by applying a thin finishing coat of actual plaster to the grey face. The plastering is not easy for the inexperienced but with some practice you could tackle your walls. Ceilings should be left to professionals though you can prepare the plasterboard and have it ready for the tradesman to plaster.

Preparing the background

First fill the gaps between the board joints and at the angles, bringing them flush with the boards. Use board-finish plaster for one-coat plastering, an undercoat first for two-coat plastering.

Reinforce all of the joints and angles with jute scrim pressed into a thin band of the plaster. Let the plaster set, but not dry out, before applying the finishing plaster.

Rolls of jute scrim 90mm (3½in) wide are available from builders' merchants.

If you intend to plaster the walls yourself, first study the section on plastering thoroughly (▷).

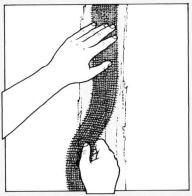

Reinforce joints with scrim before plastering

Decorating direct

Before the ivory side of plasterboard can be directly decorated it must be given a uniform surface by the application of a sealer.

Brush or sponge-apply a thin coating of finish mixed to a thin consistency. If applying it by brush, follow it up with the sponge worked in a light circular motion over the entire surface. Alternatively, use a proprietary ready-mixed top coat which can be applied with a brush or roller and is suitable for all decorative treatments. Two coats will also provide a vapour barrier.

PLASTERBOARDING A CEILING

A new ceiling may be made with plasterboard which can also be used to replace on old lath and plaster ceiling which is beyond repair.

Fixing the plasterboard in place and finishing its surface ready for direct decoration can be tackled by the non-professional, but wet plastering over a boarded ceiling should be left to the skilled tradesman as it is hard work and difficult to do well.

Preparing an old ceiling

Start by stripping away all the old damaged plaster and laths, and pull out all the nails.

This is a messy job, so wear protective clothing, a pair of goggles and a face mask while working. It's also a good idea to seal the gaps round doors in the room to prevent dust escaping through the rest of the house.

If necessary, trim back the top edge of the wall plaster so that the edge of the ceiling plasterboard can be tucked in.

Inspect and treat the exposed joists for any signs of woodworm (◁).

FITTING NEW BOARDING

Measure the area of ceiling and select the most economical size of boards to cover it.

The boards should be fitted with their long paper-covered edges running at right angles to the joists. The butting joints between the ends of boards should be staggered on each row and supported by a joist in every case.

Fit perimeter noggings between the joists against the walls and other intermediate ones in lines across the ceilings to support the long edges of the boards. It is not always necessary to fit intermediate supports if the boards are finally to be plastered, but they will ensure a sound ceiling. The intermediate noggings should be at least 50mm (2in) thick and should be fitted so that the edges of the boards will fall along their centre lines.

If necessary trim the length of the boards to ensure that their ends fall on the centre lines of the joists.

Start fixing the boards working from one corner of the room. It takes two people to support a large sheet of plasterboard while it is being fixed. Smaller sizes may be fixed single-handed, but even then a temporary wooden prop to hold them in place during nailing will be useful.

Using galvanized plasterboard nails, fix the first board, working from the joist nearest its centre and nailing at 150mm (6in) centres. This is to prevent the boards sagging in the middle, which can happen if their edges are nailed first.

Fix all the remaining boards in the same way.

If the boards are to be plastered leave 3mm (1/8in) gaps between the cut ends and the paper-covered edges. For direct decoration butt the paper-covered edges but leave 3mm (1/8in) gaps at the ends of the boards.

Finish the joints by the method described for plasterboard walls (◁).

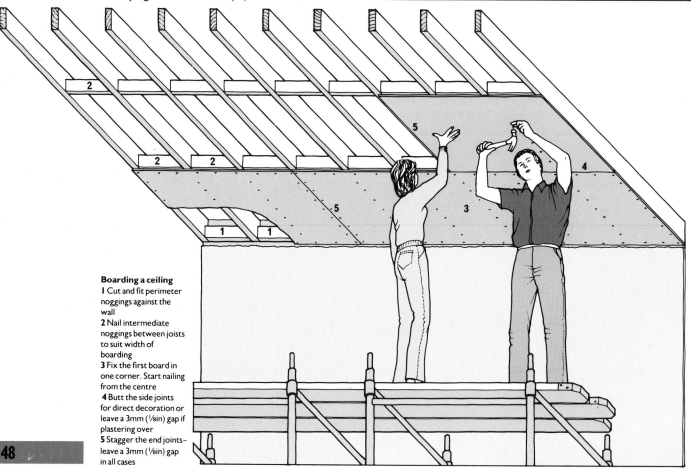

Boarding a ceiling
1 Cut and fit perimeter noggings against the wall
2 Nail intermediate noggings between joists to suit width of boarding
3 Fix the first board in one corner. Start nailing from the centre
4 Butt the side joints for direct decoration or leave a 3mm (1/8in) gap if plastering over
5 Stagger the end joints – leave a 3mm (1/8in) gap in all cases

Coving

Plaster coving is used to cover cracks in the angles between ceilings and walls, and to provide a decorative finish to plastering. It has a gypsum plaster core, moulded into a curved section, and is covered with a thick paper. Two sizes are commonly available in various lengths, with girths (widths) of 127mm (5in) and 100mm (4in).

Templates are provided by the makers to be used as guides for cutting the internal and external mitre joints.

Fitting coving

Start by marking parallel lines along the wall and ceiling, setting them off from the angle at the distance specified in the manufacturer's instructions, then scratch the plastered surfaces within the lines in order to provide a good key for the adhesive (1).

Take the measurements of the wall, then measure out the coving and cut it to fit, using the template to cut the mitres (See right). Remember that when you are cutting mitres for outside corners the coving must be longer than the wall, and must extend up to the line of the return angle drawn on the ceiling. Cut the coving with a fine-toothed saw, sawing from the face side, then lightly sandpaper the cut edges of the paper lining until smooth.

Prepare the adhesive by mixing the powder with clean water and stirring it to a creamy consistency. The adhesive should remain usable for about 30 minutes, but it's best to aim at making just enough for one length of coving.

With a filling knife apply the adhesive liberally to the back faces of the coving which will be in contact with the wall and ceiling.

Dry, bare plaster must be dampened just before the coving is put in place. Press it into the angle and level it with the guide lines (2). If a piece of coving is more than about 2m (6ft 6in) long two people should fit it. Should it tend to sag when in place support it with a couple of nails driven temporarily into the wall under its bottom edge and remove them when the adhesive has set.

Scrape away any squeezed-out beads of surplus adhesive before it sets and use it to fill the mitre joints as the work progresses. Use your finger to apply the adhesive to internal mitres if you find it easier, but finish off with a filling knife to leave a good sharp corner (3).

Wipe along the edges of the coving with a damp brush or sponge to remove any traces of adhesive. When it dries prime the coving for painting.

CUTTING THE MITRES

Using a template

The makers of plaster coving supply a cardboard template with their product which enables you to cut mitred corners more easily.

Mark the coving to length on one edge, bearing in mind whether you are mitring for an external corner or an internal one. Trim and fold the template and place it over the coving in line with the measured mark, then press it down so that it moulds itself to the curve of the material. Use the appropriate edge of the template – for an external or an internal mitre – and with a soft pencil draw the cutting line along it on the face and edges of the coving, tracing the template's edge.

Cut the mitre with a fine-toothed saw, following the marked angle.

Using a jig

If you plan to use plaster coving right through the house it will be worthwhile to make a mitre block as a jig for cutting the joints accurately.

Cut a baseboard from 18mm (¾in) plywood or chipboard about 200mm (8in) wide and 450mm (1ft 6in) long. Cut a piece of 100 x 50mm (4 x 2in) planed softwood to the same length for a fence.

Glue the fence to the baseboard flush with one long edge. When the adhesive has set mark out and make three saw cuts, one at right angles to the face of the fence and two at 45 degrees in opposite directions. Nail a stop batten to the baseboard at a distance from the fence which will allow the coving to fit snugly between them for cutting.

The baseboard of the mitre block represents the ceiling and the fence represents the wall. Lay the coving in the jig with the end to be cut in the right direction for either an external or an internal mitre (See right).

SEE ALSO

Details for: ▷
Gypsum plaster 35

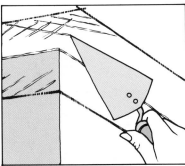
Fitted coving at external and internal corner

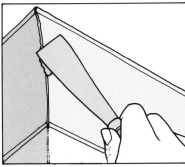
1 Scratch surface between marked lines

2 Press the coving into angle, level with the lines

3 Finish off with a filling knife

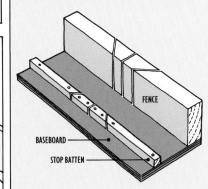
Make a mitre block for cutting joints accurately

BASEBOARD
STOP BATTEN
FENCE

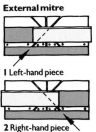

External mitre

1 Left-hand piece

2 Right-hand piece

Internal mitre

1 Left-hand piece

2 Right-hand piece

FLOORS: SUSPENDED FLOORS

Floor construction in most buildings is based on timber beams known as joists. These are rectangular in section, placed on edge for maximum strength, usually about 400mm (1ft 4in) apart, and supported at the ends by the walls.

Such 'suspended floors' contrast with the concrete 'solid floors' – supported over their whole area by the ground –

which are usually to be found in basements, and commonly at ground level in modern houses.

Traditional suspended floors are usually boarded with tongued and grooved or plain-edged planks, though in modern houses flooring-grade chipboard is now being used on both types of floor.

Ground floors

The joists of a suspended ground floor are usually made from 100 x 50mm (4 x 2in) sawn softwood. Their ends and centre portions are nailed on to supporting lengths of 100 x 75mm (4 x 3in) softwood called wall plates, and these distribute the load from the joists to the walls, which, in turn, support them.

In traditional houses various methods have been used for supporting the wall plates. At one time it was common for the ends of the joists to be slotted into the walls and set on wall plates that were built into the brickwork. Alternatively the brickwork was formed to provide ledges – called offsets – to support the wall plates. But despite damp-proof courses being laid under the wall plates of these mortar bed joists the wood was vulnerable to timber

decay caused by rising and penetrating damp in the brickwork.

The relatively lightweight joists tend to sag in the middle and are therefore generally supported by further wall plates set on three or four courses of honeycombed brickwork known as sleeper walls. The spaces in the brickwork are left so that air can circulate under the floor. Sleeper walls are usually spaced at intervals of about 2m (6ft), and are now also used to support the ends of the joists.

Beneath a fireplace in a room with a suspended floor will be found a solid brick wall, built to the same height as the sleeper walls, for retaining and supporting the concrete hearth. This fender wall carries a wall plate along its top edge to support the ends of the floor joists that run up to it.

UPPER FLOORS

Obviously the first-floor joists and those of other upper floors can be supported only at their ends, so they are usually laid in the direction of the shortest span. Also, as they can have no intermediate support, such joists are cut deeper to give them greater rigidity. These 'bridging joists' are usually 50mm (2in) thick, but their depth will be determined by the distance they must span. The joists supporting the floor of an average-size upper room would be about 225mm (9in) deep.

Where floor joists cannot run right through – as around a fireplace or at a stairway opening – a thicker joist is used to bear the extra load of the short joists. This load is transferred to the thicker joist by crosspieces jointed at right angles (See left). The thicker joists are 'trimming joists', the short ones parallel to them are 'trimmed joists' and the crosspieces joining them together are 'trimmer joists'.

In older properties the upstairs joists may be supported on wall plates which are built into solid walls; the problem of damp is less critical here. With modern cavity wall construction the ends of the joists may also be built in, but in this case they rest directly on the blockwork inner skin. The joist-ends must not project into the cavity itself, and they must be treated with a preservative to guard against the risk of timber decay (See opposite).

Suspended ground and first floors
The floor joists of a traditionally built floor are supported by wall plates and are tenon and housing jointed where one member meets another.

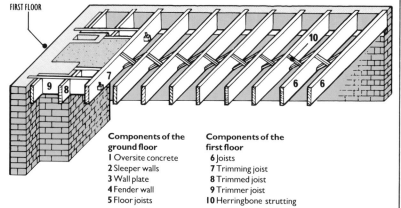

FIRST FLOOR

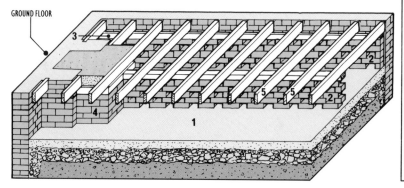

GROUND FLOOR

Components of the ground floor
1 Oversite concrete
2 Sleeper walls
3 Wall plate
4 Fender wall
5 Floor joists

Components of the first floor
6 Joists
7 Trimming joist
8 Trimmed joist
9 Trimmer joist
10 Herringbone strutting

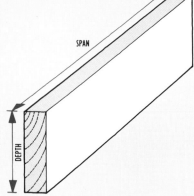

SPAN

DEPTH

To estimate the size of timber for a floor joist use the following rule of thumb as a guide.

Depth in units of 25mm (1in) =

$$\frac{\text{Span of joist in units of 300mm (1ft)}}{2} + 2$$

Examples:

● **Metric.**

Joists span 3m divided by 300mm = <u>10 units</u>

$$\frac{10 \text{ units}}{2} + 2 = 5 + 2 = 7 \text{ units} \times 25\text{mm} = \underline{175\text{mm}}$$

● **Imperial.**

$$\frac{\text{Joist span 10ft}}{2} + 2 = 5 + 2 = \underline{7 \text{ inches}}$$

BRACING FLOORS

For extra stiffness the joists of an upper floor are braced with 'solid strutting', solid sections of timber nailed between them (**1**), or with 'herringbone strutting', diagonal wooden braces (**2**).

The traditional herringbone strutting, of 50 x 25mm (2 x 1in) softwood, is preferable because it can compensate for timber shrinkage. Folded wedges or packing blocks are placed in line with the strutting between the outer joists and the walls to keep the joints tight.

In modern floor construction herringbone strutting is carried out with ready-made metal units (**3**), usually equipped with a drilled flange at each end for nailing between joists set at 400, 450 or 600mm (1ft 4in, 1ft 8in or 2ft) centres.

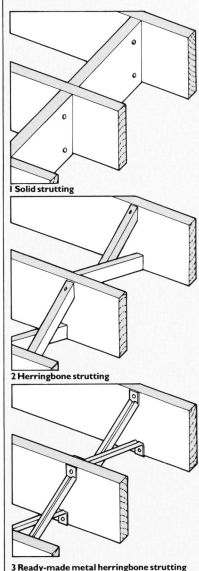

1 Solid strutting

2 Herringbone strutting

3 Ready-made metal herringbone strutting

SOLID GROUND FLOORS

Though solid floors are to be seen at all levels in large industrial buildings, in domestic houses they are normally ground floors or basements.

A solid ground floor is essentially a concrete slab laid on a sub-stratum of coarse rubble, or hardcore. To lay such a floor the topsoil is first removed and the hardcore then laid to consolidate the ground and level up the site. The rough surface of the hardcore is filled (blinded) with a thin layer of sand which is rolled flat. This sand layer prevents the cement draining out of the concrete and into the hardcore, which would cause the concrete to be weakened.

The concrete slab is usually about 100-150mm (4 to 6in) thick and is either laid over or covered by a continuous layer of moisture-resistant material, the damp-proof membrane, or DPM. The membrane may be a sheet of heavy-weight polythene – this is commonly used in modern houses – or the more traditional liquid coating of bituminous or asphalt material. The DPM, whether it is laid under or over the concrete slab, or sandwiched within it, is joined to the damp-proof course (DPC) set in the walls.

A concrete raft foundation can form a solid floor on which the walls are built, or, where strip or trench foundations are used, the slab can be laid over the ground contained within the brickwork walls.

If a floor covering is to be laid directly onto a concrete floor the floor must first be covered with a screed of sand and cement, and the screed brought to a good smooth finish. No screed is needed before laying quarry tiles if the tiles are laid with mortar rather than a proprietory tile adhesive.

Where the DPM is below the concrete slab the screed can be 45mm (1¾in) thick, but where a membrane is laid over the slab the screed should be at least 63mm (2½in) in thickness.

SEE ALSO

Details for: ▷	
Metal fittings	52
Solid floors	53

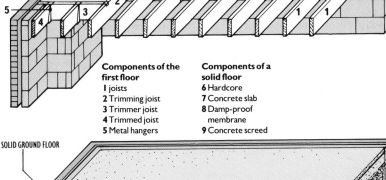

FIRST FLOOR

Components of the first floor
1 joists
2 Trimming joist
3 Trimmer joist
4 Trimmed joist
5 Metal hangers

Components of a solid floor
6 Hardcore
7 Concrete slab
8 Damp-proof membrane
9 Concrete screed

Suspended floor
The construction of a modern suspended floor is similar to the traditional method but the ends of the joists are supported by the inner blocks of the cavity wall or by metal hangers. Metal fittings such as straps and framing anchors may also be used to join the timbers to themselves or to the walls.

SOLID GROUND FLOOR

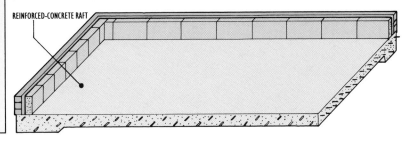

REINFORCED-CONCRETE RAFT

Solid floors
A solid floor is often used in preference to a suspended floor as it can be cheaper to construct. A concrete floor can be laid after the foundations and first courses of brickwork are built above ground level or be an integral part of a reinforced concrete foundation (See below).

METAL FITTINGS FOR FLOORS

Floor construction is one of the many areas in which modern builders have been able to substitute the use of factory-made fittings for traditional methods of construction.

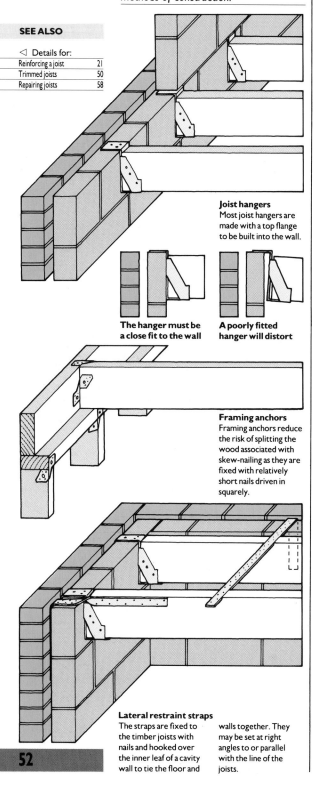

Joist hangers
Most joist hangers are made with a top flange to be built into the wall.

The hanger must be a close fit to the wall

A poorly fitted hanger will distort

Framing anchors
Framing anchors reduce the risk of splitting the wood associated with skew-nailing as they are fixed with relatively short nails driven in squarely.

Lateral restraint straps
The straps are fixed to the timber joists with nails and hooked over the inner leaf of a cavity wall to tie the floor and walls together. They may be set at right angles to or parallel with the line of the joists.

Joist hangers

Galvanized steel joist hangers are now in wide use in the construction of upper timber floors. These are brackets which are fastened to walls to support the ends of the joists. There are various versions for securing to solid or cavity walls and for constructing timber-to-timber joints.

The use of metal joist hangers allows brickwork or blockwork to be completely built up before the joists are fitted. It also saves the awkward infilling between joists that is necessary when the ends of the joists are built into the inner leaf of the walls.

The hangers must be fitted properly, with the top flange sitting squarely on the surface of the brickwork. Any packing that is used must cover the whole bearing surface and must be as strong in compression as the masonry. The rear face of the bracket must fully meet the face of the brickwork.

The ends of the joists are fixed into hangers with 32mm (1 1/4in) sherardized twisted nails or plasterboard nails, one or two being driven through the holes in the side gussets.

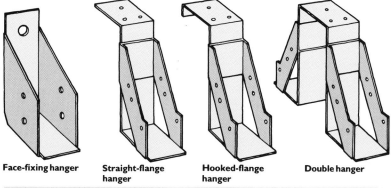

Face-fixing hanger	**Straight-flange hanger**	**Hooked-flange hanger**	**Double hanger**

Framing anchors

Framing anchors are steel brackets which are used to make butt joints with timbers. They are in growing use among builders to fix trimmed joists instead of the traditional – and time-consuming – tenon and housing joints.

Framing anchors are made left- and right-handed

Lateral restraint straps

While the walls carry the weight of the floor, the floor adds to the lateral stiffness of the walls. In areas where the force of the wind can threaten the stability of modern lightweight walls, lateral restraint straps are used to provide ties between the walls and the floor. They are simply stiff strips of galvanized steel, perforated for nail fixing and bent in various ways to suit the direction of the joists.

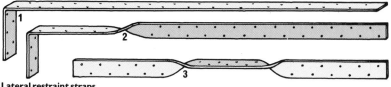

Lateral restraint straps
1 For tying joists parallel to an external wall
2 For tying joists at right angles to an external wall
3 For tying joists on either side of an internal wall

BOARDED SOLID FLOORS

Most floor coverings, including wooden block flooring, can be bonded directly to a dry, smooth screeded floor, but floorboards cannot be directly bonded and so must be fixed by other means.

The boards are nailed down to 50 x 50mm (2 x 2in) softwood battens, or bearers. The battens are embedded in the concrete while it is wet or are later fixed to clips which have been embedded. In either case the timber must be treated with a wood preservative. A damp-proof membrane (DPM) must be incorporated, usually in the form of a continuous coat of bituminous material sandwiched within the slab. A smooth finished screed is unnecessary under a boarded floor.

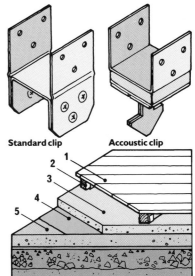

Standard clip   **Accoustic clip**

SEE ALSO

Details for: ▷
Flooring   54

The clip method

This means of fixing requires the slab to be level and relatively smooth. The flanges of the clips are pressed into the surface of the concrete before it sets, while a marked guide batten is used to space the clips and align them in rows. The rows are normally set 400mm (1ft 4in) apart to centres starting 50mm (2in) from one wall. When the concrete is completely dry the 'ears' of the clips are raised from their folded position with a claw hammer. The battens, having been cut to length and their ends treated with a preservative, are nailed in place through the holes in the clips. The boards are nailed to the battens.

I Clip method
Composition of floor
1 Floorboards
2 Clipped battens
3 Concrete screed
4 DPM
5 Concrete slab

Embedded battens

These are splayed in section so as to key into the concrete slab. Again, the slab is built up in two layers with the damp-proof membrane sandwiched between them. Before the top layer is laid the treated battens are positioned at 400mm (1ft 4in) centres and levelled on dabs of concrete. Strips of wood are nailed across them temporarily to hold them in position. When the dabs of concrete are set and the battens firmly held, the wood strips are removed and the top layer of concrete is poured and compacted. It is levelled with a rule, notched to fit over the battens, which is drawn along them and finishes the concrete 12mm (½in) below their tops. When the concrete layer is fully dry the boards are nailed on the battens in the conventional way.

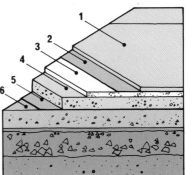

2 Embedded battens
Composition of floor
1 Floorboards
2 Embedded battens
3 Concrete screed
4 DPM
5 Concrete slab

Chipboard floating floors

Flooring grade chipboard is a relatively recent innovation as a material for boarding over a solid floor. It is quicker and cheaper to lay a chipboard floor than one made of boards. It is also more stable and it can be laid without being fixed to the concrete slab.

It produces a floor of the type known as a 'floating floor'. The simplest floor of this kind is laid with 18mm (¾in) tongued and grooved chipboard, either the standard grade or the moisture-resistant type (▷).

First a sheet of insulating material such as rigid polystyrene or fibre board is laid on the concrete slab; then, normally, a vapour barrier of polythene sheet is laid above the polystyrene. The vapour barrier must be a continuous sheet, with its edges turned up and trapped behind the skirting boards. The chipboard, its edges glued, is then laid on the vapour barrier.

The chipboard flooring is held in place by its own weight, but is also trapped by the skirting boards, which are nailed to the walls round its edges. The skirting boards also cover a 10mm (⅜in) gap between the chipboard and the walls, allowing for expansion across the floor.

3 Chipboard floating floor
Composition of floor
1 Chipboard flooring
2 Vapour check
3 Polystyrene insulation
4 Concrete screed
5 DPM
6 Concrete Slab

Battened floating floor

Battens can be incorporated in a floating floor. Lengths of 50 x 50mm (2 x 2in) softwood, treated with a preservative, are used. They are spaced at 400mm (1ft 4in) intervals for the 18mm (¾in) chipboard; for the heavier gauge 22mm (⅞in) material they are spaced 600mm (2ft) apart.

A quilt-type sheet of insulating material is laid on the concrete slab, then covered with a polythene vapour barrier. The battens are positioned on the insulation, held together temporarily with strips of wood nailed across them. Tongued and grooved chipboard flooring is laid at right angles to the battens, the edges being glued before it is nailed down.

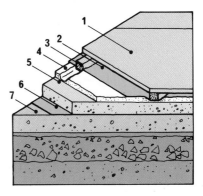

4 Battened floating floor
Composition of floor
1 Chipboard flooring
2 Vapour check
3 Battens
4 Insulation
5 Concrete screed
6 DPM
7 Concrete slab

53

FLOORING

Flooring is the general term used to describe the boarding which is laid over the floor's structural elements – the timber floor joists or the concrete slab.

This boarding can consist of hardwood or softwood planks, or it can be constructed with manufactured boards of plywood or chipboard.

Floorboards

Softwoods are generally used for making floorboards. The standard sizes are 125 x 25mm (5 x 1in) or 150 x 25mm (6 x 1in) nominal (◁). They are sold planed all round (PAR) with square edges or tongued and grooved ones. Their thicknesses range between 22mm (⅞in) and less commonly 32mm (1¼in).

However, boards as narrow as 90mm (3½in) and others as wide as 280mm (11in) may be found in some houses. The narrow boards produce superior floors because they make any movement due to shrinkage less noticeable. But installing them is costly in labour, and they are used only in expensive houses. Hardwoods, such as oak or maple, are also used for high-grade floor construction but are not common due to their high cost.

The best floorboards are quarter sawn (**1**) from the log, a method that diminishes distortion from shrinkage. But as this method is wasteful of timber, boards are more often cut tangentially (**2**) for reasons of economy. Boards cut

in this way tend to bow, or 'cup' across their width and they should be fixed with the cupped side facing upwards, as there is a tendency for the grain of the other side to splinter. The cut of a board – tangential or quarter cut – can be checked by looking at the annual growth rings on the end grain.

The joint of tongued and grooved boards is not at the centre of their edges but closer to one face, and these boards should be laid with the offset joint nearer to the joist. Though tongued and grooved boards are nominally the same sizes as square edged boards the edge joint reduces their floor coverage by about 12mm (½in) per board.

In some old buildings you may find floorboards bearing the marks left by an adze on their undersides. Such old boards have usually been trimmed to a required thickness only where they sit over the joists, while their top faces and edges are planed smooth.

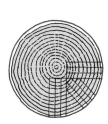

1 Quarter-sawn boards
Shrinkage does not distort these boards

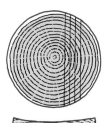

2 Tangentially-sawn boards
Shrinkage can cause these boards to 'cup'

SHEET FLOORING

Softwood and hardwood boards not only provide a tough flooring; when sealed and polished they will also take on an attractive colour. But sheet materials such as flooring grade plywood or chipboard are merely functional, and are used as a sub-base for other floor surfaces.

Plywood

Any exterior grade plywood – known in the trade as WPB bonded plywood – can be used for flooring. Those sold as flooring grade plywoods are tongued and grooved on two or all four edges.

Plywood flooring laid directly over the joists should be 16 to 18mm (⅝ to ¾in) thick, though boards laid over an existing floor surface, to level it or to provide an underlay for tiles, can be 6 to 12mm (¼ to ½in) in thickness. Plywood floors are laid in the same way as chipboard ones.

Chipboard

Only proper flooring grade chipboard, which is compressed to a higher density than the standard material, should be used for flooring. It is available in square-edged and tongued and grooved boards. The square-edged boards measure 2.4 x 1.22m (8 x 4ft) and are 18mm (¾in) thick. Tongued and grooved boards are available in two grades: the standard Type II and the moisture-resistant Type II/III. Both grades come in sheets measuring 2.4m x 600mm (8 x 2ft) and 22mm (⅞in) thick. The moisture-resistant type should always be used where damp conditions may occur, such as in bathrooms or kitchens.

The 18mm (¾in) thick boards are suitable for laying on joists spaced no more than 400mm (1ft 4in) apart. Where the joists are at 600mm (2ft) intervals the 22mm (⅞in) boarding must be used.

Types of flooring
1 Square-edged chipboard
2 T and G chipboard
3 T and G plywood
4 T and G softwood boards
5 Square-edged softwood boards
6 T and G hardwood boards

TONGUED AND GROOVED BOARDING

You can detect whether your floorboards are tongued and grooved by trying to push a knife blade into the gap between them.

To lift a tongued and grooved board it is necessary first to cut through the tongue on each side of the board. Saw carefully along the line of the joint with a dovetail or tenon saw (1) held at a shallow angle. A straight batten temporarily nailed along the edge of the board may help you to keep the saw on a straight line.

With the tongue cut through, saw across the board and lift it as you would a plain-edged one.

If the original flooring has been 'secret nailed' (2), use lost head nails (3) to fix the boards back in place and conceal the recesses with a matching wood filler.

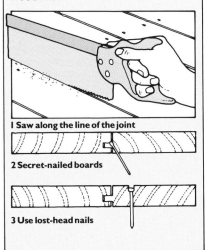

1 Saw along the line of the joint

2 Secret-nailed boards

3 Use lost-head nails

REFITTING A CUT BOARD

The butted ends of floorboards normally meet and rest on a joist (1) and a board which has been cut flush with the side of a joist must be given a new means of support when replaced (2).

Cut a piece of 50 x 50mm (2 x 2in) softwood and screw it to the side of the joists flush with the top. Screw the end of the floorboard to the support.

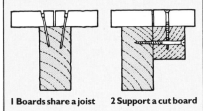

1 Boards share a joist   2 Support a cut board

LIFTING FLOORBOARDS

Floorboarding is produced in lengths that are intended to run from wall to wall. In practice this is rarely carried out entirely because odd, shorter lengths are often laid to save on materials.

When lifting floorboards it is these shorter pieces that you should start with if possible. In many older homes one or two boards will probably have been lifted already for access to services.

Square-edged boards

Tap the blade of a bolster (▷) into the gap between the boards close to the cut end (1). Lever up the edge of the board but try not to crush the edge of the one next to it. Fit the bolster into the gap at the other side of the board and repeat the procedure. Ease the end of the board up in this way, then work the claw of a hammer under it until you can lift it enough to slip a cold chisel (▷) under it (2). Move along the board to the next set of nails and proceed in the same way, continuing until the board comes away.

1 Lever up board with bolster chisel

2 Place cold chisel under board

Lifting a continuous board

Floorboards are nailed in place before the skirting boards are fixed, so the ends of a continuous board are trapped under them. If you need to lift such a board it will have to be cut.

Ease up the centre of the board with the bolster so that its full thickness is clear of the adjacent boards, then slip the cold chisel under it to keep it bowed (1). Remove the nails, and with a tenon saw cut through the board over the centre of the joist. You can then lift the two halves of the board using the same method as for a short one.

Boards that are too stiff to be bowed upwards, or are tongued and grooved, will have to be cut across in situ. This means cutting flush with the side of the joist instead of over its centre.

Locate the side of the joist by passing the blade of a padsaw (2) vertically into the gaps on both sides of the board (the joints of tongued and grooved boards will also have to be cut (See left). Mark the edges of the board where the blade stops, and draw a line between these points representing the side of the joist. Make a starting hole for the saw blade by drilling three or four 3mm (⅛in) holes close together at one end of the line marked across the surface.

Work the tip of the blade into the hole and start making the cut with short strokes. Gradually tip the blade to a shallow angle to avoid cutting into any cables or pipes that may be hidden below. Lever up the board with a bolster chisel as described above.

Freeing the end of a board

The end of the board trapped under the skirting can usually be freed by being lifted to a steep angle, when the 50mm (2in) gap between the joists and the wall should allow the board to clear the nails and be pulled free (1).

To raise a floorboard that runs beneath a partition wall, the board must also be cut close to the wall. Drill a starting hole and then cut the board as close to the wall as possible (2).

There is a special saw (3) that can be used for cutting floorboards. It has a curved cutting edge that allows you to cut a board without fully lifting it.

SEE ALSO

Details for: ▷
Bolster   78
Cold chisel   78

1 Saw across the board

2 Find the joist's side

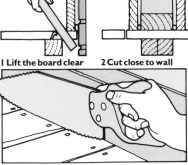

1 Lift the board clear   2 Cut close to wall

3 Hire a floorboard saw if necessary

RE-LAYING A FLOOR

Though floors probably take more wear and tear than any other interior surface this is not usually the reason why re-laying boarding becomes necessary. Fire damage or timber decay – which would also affect the joists – or simply large gaps in the boarding caused by shrinkage may require the floor to be re-laid, or even entirely renewed.

If the floor is to be renewed, measure the room and buy your materials in advance. Leave floorboards or sheets of chipboard to acclimatise – ideally in the room where they are to be laid – for at least a week before fixing.

Removing the flooring

To lift the complete flooring you must first remove the skirting boards from the walls (◁). If you intend to re-lay the boards, number them with chalk before starting to raise them. Lift the first few boards as described (◁), starting from one side of the room, then prise up the remainder by working a cold chisel or crowbar between the joists and the undersides of the boards. In the case of tongued and grooved boards, two or three should be eased up simultaneously, to avoid breaking the joints, and progressively pulled away.

Pull all the nails out of the boards and joists, and scrape any accumulated dirt from the tops of the joists. Clean the edges of the boards similarly if they are to be re-used. Check all timbers for rot or insect infestation and treat or repair them as required.

● **Treating timber**
Treat woodworm-infested and rotten woodwork by brushing or spraying with an all-purpose chemical preservative. The same preservative will protect new timber.

● **Closing gaps**
You can re-lay floorboards without removing all the boards at once. Lift and re-nail about six boards at a time as you work across the floor. Finally cut and fit a new board to fill the last gap.

Laying the boards
Working from a platform of loose boards, proceed in the following order
1 Fix first board parallel to the wall
2 Cut and lay up to six boards, cramp them together and nail
3 Lay the next group of boards in the same way, continue across the floor and cut the last board to fit

Laying new floorboards

Though the following deals with fixing tongued and grooved floorboarding, the basic method described applies equally to square-edged boarding.

Lay a few loose boards together to form a work platform. Measure the width or length of the room – whichever is at right angles to the joists – and cut your boards to stop 10mm (⅜in) short of the walls at each end. Where two shorter boards are to be butted end to end, cut them so that the joint will be centred on a joist and set the boards out so as to avoid such joins occurring on the same joist with adjacent boards. Any two butt joints must be separated by at least one whole board. Lay four to six boards at a time.

Fix the first board with its grooved edge no more than 10mm (⅜in) from the wall and nail it in place with cut floor brads or lost-head nails that are at least twice as long as the thickness of the floorboard.

Place the nails in pairs, one about 25mm (1in) from each edge of the board and centred on the joists. Punch them in about 2mm (¹/₁₆in). Place one nail in the tongued edge if secret nailing.

Lay the other cut boards in place and cramp them up to the fixed one so as to close the edge joints. Special floorboard cramps can be hired for this, but wedges cut from 400mm (1ft 4in) off-cuts of board will work just as well **(1)**. To cramp the boards with wedges, temporarily nail another board just less than a board's width away from them. Insert the pairs of wedges in the gap, resting on every fourth or fifth joist, and with two hammers tap the wedges' broad ends toward each other. Nail the cramped-up boards in place as before, then remove the wedges and temporary board and repeat the operation with the next group of boards, continuing in this way across the room.

At the far wall place the remaining boards, cutting the last one to width, its tongue on the 'waste' side. It should be cut to leave a gap equal to the width of the tongue or 12mm (½in), whichever is less. If you cannot get the last board to slot in, cut away the bottom section of the grooved edge so that it will drop into place **(2)**.

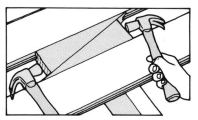

1 Make wedges to cramp boards

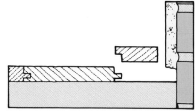

2 Cut away part of last board's grooved edge

FLOORBOARD CRAMP

This special tool automatically grips the joist over which it is placed by means of two toothed cams. A screw-operated ram applies pressure to the floorboards when the tommy bar is turned.

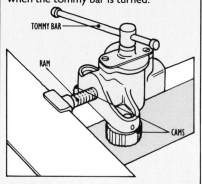

TOMMY BAR

RAM

CAMS

LAYING CHIPBOARD FLOORING

For a floor that is going to be invisible beneath some kind of covering – vinyl, cork, fitted carpet or whatever – chipboard is an excellent material. It is laid relatively quickly and is much cheaper than an equivalent amount of timber flooring. It comes square-edged or tongued and grooved. Each has its own laying technique.

CUTTING TO FIT

Square-edge boards
The widths of the boards may have to be cut down (1) so that their long edges will butt on the joists' centre lines.
Tongued and grooved boards
Only the last boards need be cut in their width (2) to fit against the wall.

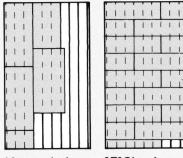

1 Square-edged boards

2 T&G boards

Square-edged boards

All the edges of square-edged chipboard flooring must be supported. Lay the boards with their long edges along the joists and nail 75 x 50mm (3 x 2in) softwood noggings between the joists to support the boards' ends. The noggings against the wall can be placed in advance; those supporting joints between boards must be nailed into place as the boards are laid.

Start with a full-length board in one corner and lay a row of boards the length of the room, cutting the last one to fit as required. Leave an expansion gap of about 10mm (⅜in) between the outer edges of the boards and the walls. If the boards' inner edges do not fall on the centre line of a joist, cut them down so that they do so on the nearest one, but cut the surplus off the outer edge, near the wall.

Nail the boards down close together, using 50mm (2in) or 56mm (2¼in) annular ring nails spaced about 300mm (1ft) apart along the joists and noggings. Place the nails about 18mm (¾in) from the edges.

Cut and lay the remainder of the boards with the end joints staggered on alternate rows.

Tongued and grooved boards

Tongued and grooved boards are laid with their long edges running across the joists. Noggings are needed only against the walls, to support the outer edges. The ends of the boards are supported by joists.

Working from one corner, lay the first board with its grooved edges about 10mm (⅜in) from the walls and nail it into place.

Apply PVA wood adhesive to the joint along the end of the first board, then lay the next one in the row. Knock it up to the first board with a hammer for a good close joint, protecting the edge with a piece of scrap wood. Nail the board down as before, then wipe any surplus adhesive from the surface before it sets, using a damp rag. Continue in this way across the floor, gluing all of the joints as you go. Cut boards to fit at the ends of rows or to fall on the centre of a joist as and stagger these end joints on alternate rows.

Finally fit the skirting, which will cover the expansion gaps.

You can seal the surface of the chipboard with two coats of clear polyurethane varnish if you wish, to protect it from dirt.

SEE ALSO

Details for: ▷	
Chipboard flooring	54
Fitting skirting	59

1 Square-edged boards
Lay the boards with their long edges on a joist and the ends supported with noggings.

2 Tongued and grooved boards
Lay the boards across the joists with the ends falling on a joist.

1 Arrangement for laying square-edged boards

2 Arrangement for laying T&G boards

57

FLOOR JOISTS

Fitting services
1 Make holes within the shaded line
2 Place notches within shaded area

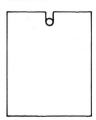

Drill and saw notches to accommodate pipe

Repairing a joist
The stages for replacing a joist are combined in the illustration.

Order of working
1 Cut away old joist
2 Cut out wall plate
3 Fit new wall plate
4 Cut and fit new joist and brace the joint with bolted joist timbers

Floor joists are important structural elements of a house. Being load-bearing, their size and spacing in new structures is strictly specified by the Building Regulations and they must satisfy a Building Control Officer. But for most domestic repairs or replacements the rule of thumb guide (◁) is adequate. Usually calculations are not necessary; matching new timber for old in size should suffice.

Use 'structurally graded' timber; it has been expertly examined or machine tested. Two common grades are marked with coloured code letters. A purple SS is the grade mark of 'special structural timber', used for joists. A green GS indicates 'general structural timber', for general framing but also joists. MSS and MGS denote machine-graded timber to the same specification.

Fitting services

Service runs like heating pipes and electric cables can run in the void below a suspended ground floor, but those running at right angles to the joists in upper floors must pass through the joists, which are covered by flooring above and a ceiling below.

So as not to weaken joists the holes for cables should centre on the joist's depth, in any event at least 50mm (2in) below the top surface to clear floor nails, and always within the middle two thirds of the joist's length **(1)** .

Notches for pipe runs in the top edge should be no deeper than one eighth the depth of the joist and within a quarter of the joist's length at each end **(2)** . Make notches by drilling through the joist, then sawing down to the hole.

Repairing joists

Floor joists which have been seriously attacked by wet rot, dry rot or insect infestation have to be cut out and replaced. Such attack usually occurs at ground floor level because of its closeness to the damp soil. If the damage is extensive, or if the upper floors are also affected, you should really call in an expert, but if it is localised and not too serious you can deal with it yourself.

Remove the skirtings and lift the floorboards over the infected area until you reach a sleeper wall (◁). Test the condition of the wood – joists, floorboards and skirting boards – by spiking it with a sharp knife. If the blade penetrates easily the wood will have to be replaced. Sound wood can be chemically treated to kill rot spores or wood-boring insect larvae (◁).

Preparation

The damp conditions which have caused the outbreak of wet or dry rot must themselves be identified and corrected before any remedial work on the timbers is carried out.

All infected timbers must be removed in an area extending at least 450mm (1ft 6in) beyond the last visible signs of attack, and all surrounding masonry must be treated with a fungicide (◁). Burn all the infected timber. The following assumes that the end of a joist and perhaps also the wall plate are affected.

Saw through and remove the infected end of the joist, cutting it back to the centre of the nearest sleeper wall. If the wall plate which has been supporting

the joist is also affected, cut it away. If the wall plate is built into the brickwork, drill a series of holes into its edge and finish cutting it away with a wood chisel and mallet, trimming the remaining ends square. Wall plates on sleeper walls are simply cut with a saw.

Replacement

Cut a new length of wall plate timber to fill the gap and treat it thoroughly with wood preservative.

If the original mortar bed joint and damp-proof course are undamaged, apply a coating of liquid bituminous damp-proofing over it and put the new section of wall plate into place.

If necessary, re-lay the bed joint and insert a new length of DPC, making sure that its ends overlap the ends of the old one, if present, by at least 150mm (6in). Then reseat the wall plate.

Now cut a length of new joist to sit on the repaired wall plate and meet the cut end of the old joist on the sleeper wall. Treat it well with the timber preservative. To ensure that it is level with the other joists, trim its underside or pack it with DPC felt.

Brace the joint with two 1m (3ft) lengths of joist timber – also treated – on each side and bolt through with four coach bolts and two timber connectors for each bolt.

Finally replace the floorboards and skirtings (◁).

FITTING JOIST HANGERS

Sections of infected wall plate which have had to be removed can be replaced with metal joist hangers (◁) to support the ends of the repaired joists.

Having removed the damaged joist and section of wall plate (See above), lay bricks in the resulting slot. But before laying the cement check on the condition of the DPC and reinforce it with an extra layer of DPC felt or a liquid damp-proofing material if you think it necessary.

Set the flange of the joist hanger in mortar at the required level, then allow the mortar to harden before fitting the new section of joist as indicated above.

SKIRTINGS

Skirtings are protective 'kick boards', but are usually also moulded to form a decorative border between the floor and walls. Modern skirtings are relatively small and simply formed, with either a rounded or bevelled top edge.

Skirtings found in older houses can be as much as 300mm (1ft) wide and quite elaborately moulded, but those in most homes are about 175mm (7in) wide and of 'ovolo' or 'torus' design. These can still be bought from timber merchants. Some will supply more elaborate designs to special order.

Skirtings can be nailed directly on to plastered brickwork or to battens, known as 'grounds', which have been fixed during the plastering stage. Skirting boards on partition walls are nailed to timber studs.

Removing skirting

Remove skirting by levering it away from the wall with a crowbar or bolster chisel. Where a skirting butts against a door architrave or an external corner it can be levered off easily enough, but a continuous length whose ends are mitred into internal corners will have to be cut before it can be removed.

Tap the blade of the bolster between the skirting and the wall, and lever the top edge away sufficiently to insert the chisel end of the crowbar behind it. Place a thin strip of wood behind the crowbar to protect the wall, tap the bolster in again a little further on, and work along the skirting in this way as the nails loosen.

With the board removed, pull the nails out through the back to avoid splitting the face.

Cutting a long skirting
A long stretch of skirting will bend out sufficiently for you to cut it in place if you lever it away at its centre and insert blocks of wood (1), one on each side of the proposed cut, to hold the board about 25mm (1in) from the wall.

Make a vertical cut with a panel saw held at about 45 degrees to the face of the board (2) and work with short strokes, using the tip of the saw.

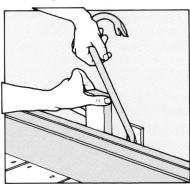

1 Prise skirting away from wall and pack out

2 Cut through skirting with tip of saw

Fitting new skirting

A skirting board can be damaged by timber decay or woodworm, or it can suffer in the process of being removed when a repair to a floor is being made. Restore the skirting if you can, especially if it is a special moulding; otherwise try to make it up from various moulded sections (See right). Standard mouldings are easily available.

Measure the length of the wall. Most skirtings are mitred at the corners, so take this into account when you are measuring between internal and external corners.

Mark the length on the plain bottom edge of the board, then mark a 45 degree angle on the edge and square it across the face of the board (▷). Fix the board on edge in a vice and carefully cut down the line at that angle.

Sometimes moulded skirtings are scribed and butt-jointed at internal corners. To achieve the profile, cut the end off one board at 45 degrees as you would for a mitre joint (1), and with a coping saw cut along the contour line on the moulded face so that it will 'jig-saw' with its neighbour (2).

Fix skirting boards with cut clasp nails when nailing to brickwork and with lost head nails when attaching them to wooden grounds.

SKIRTING MOULDINGS

Most standard skirting mouldings are made in softwood ready for painting. Hardwood is not so common and is reserved for special decorative skirting. Hardwoods are coated with a clear finish. 'Moulded-reverse' skirtings have a different profile machined on each side of the board. This provides two skirtings in one.

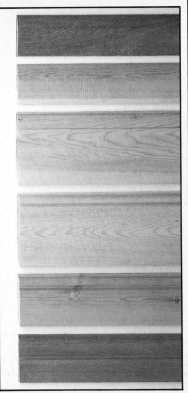

Selection of skirting mouldings
(*From top to bottom*) Bevelled hardwood. Bevelled/rounded reverse. Ovolo/bevelled reverse. Torus/bevelled reverse. Ovolo/torus reverse. Hard wood skirting.

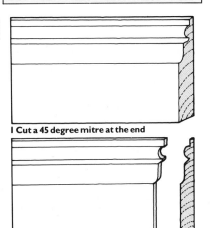

1 Cut a 45 degree mitre at the end

2 Cut the shape following the contour line

SEE ALSO

Details for: ▷

Try square	76
Panel saw	77
Coping saw	77

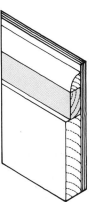

Making a skirting
If you are unable to buy a length of skirting to match your original, and the cost of having it specially machined is too high, make it up from various sections of wood.

DOORS: TYPES AND CONSTRUCTION

At first glance there appears to be a great variety of doors to choose from, but in fact most of the differences are simply stylistic. They are all based on a small number of construction methods.

The wide range of styles can sometimes tempt householders into buying doors that are inappropriate to the houses they live in. When replacing a front door you should be careful to choose one that is not incongruous with the architectural style of your house.

Buying a door

Doors in softwood and hardwood are available, the latter being the more expensive and normally used for a special interior or an entrance where the natural features of the wood can be exploited to the best effect.

Softwood doors are for more general workaday use and are intended to be painted as opposed to clear finished.

Glazed doors are becoming common features in the front and rear entrances of today's houses. They are traditionally of wooden frame construction, though modern aluminium-framed doors can be bought in the standard sizes, complete with double glazing and fitments.

Wooden framed and panel doors are supplied in unfinished wood, and these require trimming, glazing and fitting out with hinges, locks and letter plates (◁).

External flush door
A central rail is fitted to take a letter plate.

1 Planted moulding

2 Bolection moulding

DOOR SIZES

Doors are made in several standard sizes to meet most domestic needs.

The range of heights is usually 2m (6ft 6in), 2.03m (6ft 8in) and occasionally 2.17m (7ft). The widths range from 600mm (2ft) to 900mm (3ft) in steps of about 75mm (3in). Thicknesses vary from 35mm (1⅜in) to 45mm (1¾in).

In older houses it is common to find that larger doors have been used for the main room on the ground floor than for others, but modern homes tend to have standard-size joinery and all internal doors the same size. The standard is usually 2m x 762mm (6ft 6in x 2ft 6in), though front entrance doors are always larger than internal ones to suit the proportions of the building.

When replacing doors in an old house, where the openings may well be non-standard sizes, buy one of the nearest size and cut it down, removing an equal amount from each edge to preserve the frame's symmetry (◁).

Panel doors

Panel doors are stronger and more attractive than flush doors but are also more expensive. They have hardwood or softwood frames, mortise-and-tenon jointed, with grooves that house the panels, which can be of solid wood, plywood or glass.

1 Muntins
These are the central vertical members of the door. They are jointed into the three cross rails.

2 Panels
These may be of solid wood or of plywood. They are held loosely in grooves in the frame to allow for shrinkage without splitting. They stiffen the door.

3 Cross rails
Top, centre and bottom rails are tenoned into the stiles. In cheaper doors the mortise and tenon joints are replaced with dowel joints.

4 Stiles
These are the upright members at the sides of the door. They carry the hinges and door locks.

Panel door mouldings
The frame's inner edges may be plain or moulded as a decorative border. Small mouldings can be machined on the frame before assembly or pinned to the inside edge. Ordinary planted moulding (**1**) can shrink from the frame, making cracks in the paintwork. Bolection moulding (**2**) laps the frame to overcome this. It is decorative but more vulnerable.

Flush doors

Flush doors are softwood frames with plywood or hardboard covering both sides and packed with a core material. Used mainly internally, they are lightweight, cheap, simple and rather lacking in character. External ones have a central rail to take a letter plate. Firecheck doors are a special fire-retardant grade.

1 Top and bottom rails
These are tenoned into the stiles (side pieces).

2 Intermediate rails
These lighter rails, jointed to the stiles, are notched to allow passage of air and prevent the panels sinking.

3 Lock blocks
A softwood block to take a mortise lock is glued to each stile.

4 Panels
the plywood or hardboard panels are left plain for painting or finished with a wood veneer. Metal skinned doors may be had to special order.

Core material
Paper or cardboard honeycomb is sometimes sandwiched between the panels. In firecheck doors a fire-retardant material is used.

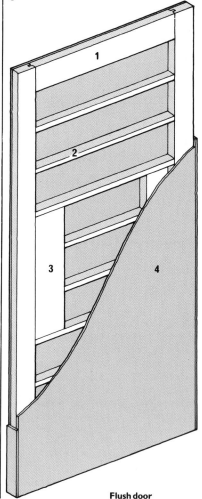

Panel door

Flush door

Ledged and braced doors

These doors have a rustic, cottagey look and are often found in old houses, out-buildings and garden walls. They are weather-resistant, strong, secure and cheap, but a little crude. A superior framed version is tenon-jointed instead of being merely nailed.

1 Battens
Tongue-and-groove boards are nailed to the ledges.

2 T-hinges
Butt hinges will not hold in the end-grain of the ledges, so long T-hinges take the weight.

3 Braces
These diagonals, notched into the ledges, transmit the weight to the hinges and stop the door sagging.

4 Ledges
These are the cross rails to which the battens are nailed.

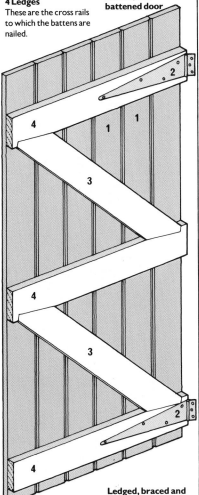

Framed, ledged, braced, and battened door

Ledged, braced and battened door

DOOR FRAMES AND CASINGS

External frames

An exterior door is fitted into a stout wooden frame consisting of the head (1) at the top, the sill (2) below, with a water-repellent weather bar, and – mortised and tenoned between them – two rebated side posts (3).

The horns, 50mm (2in) projections (4) of the head on each side, support the joints and are built into the brickwork to hold the frame in place. The pallets (5) are wooden plates, also built into the brickwork, for nail-fixing the frame.

Metal brackets (6) can provide an alternative way of fixing the door frame.

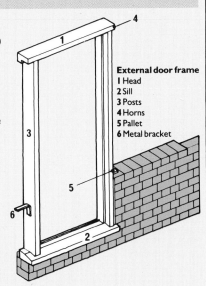

External door frame
1 Head
2 Sill
3 Posts
4 Horns
5 Pallet
6 Metal bracket

Internal casings

Internal doors are hung in a timber lining frame (See below) made up from three members: the soffit casing (1) at the top and jamb casings (2) on both sides of the opening. They are jointed together at the corners with bare-faced tongue-and-groove joints (3) as well as being nailed to pallets, wooden plugs (4) in the brickwork at 600mm (2ft) intervals. Casings may also be nail-fixed directly to block walls.

The architrave (5), plain or moulded, covers the joints and gives the casing a finish. The door closes against applied door stops (6) which form a rebate.

In better-quality buildings hardwood casings are often nailed to softwood grounds (See below). These are rough-sawn lengths of timber which are nailed in place to form a frame on each side of the door opening.

The soffit grounds (7) are nailed to the front of the lintel and the jamb grounds (8) to wooden plugs in the brickwork. They provide a level for the wall plaster and a good fixing for the architrave moulding.

Internal door casing
1 Soffit casing
2 Jamb casing
3 Bare-faced T&G joint
4 Pallet
5 Architrave
6 Door stop

Internal hardwood casing
7 Soffit grounds
8 Jamb grounds

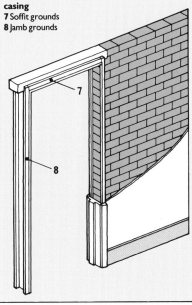

FITTING AND HANGING DOORS

Whatever the style of door you wish to fit, the procedure is the same, though minor differences between some external doors may show themselves. Two good-quality 100mm (4in) butt hinges are enough to support a standard door, but if you are hanging a heavy hardwood one you should add a third, central hinge.

All doors are fairly heavy, and as it is necessary to try a door in its frame several times to get the fit right you will find that the job goes much more quickly and easily if you have a helper working with you.

Fitting a door

Before attaching the hinges to a new door make sure that it fits nicely into its frame. It should have a clearance of 2mm (1/16in) at the top and sides and should clear the floor by at least 6mm (1/4in). As much as 12mm (1/2in) may be required for a carpeted floor.

Measure the height and width of the door opening and the depth of the rebate in the door frame into which the door must fit. Choose a door of the right thickness and, if you cannot get one that will fit the opening exactly, one which is large enough to be cut down.

Cutting to size

Some doors are supplied with 'horns', extensions to their stiles which protect the corners while the doors are in storage. Cut these off with a saw (**1**) before starting to trim the door to size.

Transfer the measurements from the frame to the door, making necessary allowance for the clearances all round. To reduce the width of the door stand it on edge with its latch stile upwards while it is steadied in a portable vice. Plane the stile down to the marked line, working only on the one side if a small amount is to be taken off. If a lot is to be removed, take some off each side. This is especially important with panel doors to preserve the symmetry.

If you need to take off more than 6mm (1/4in) to reduce the height of the door, remove it with a saw and finish off with a plane. Otherwise plane the waste off (**2**). The plane must be sharp to deal with the end grain of the stiles. Work from each corner towards the centre to avoid 'chipping out' the corners.

Try the door in the frame, supporting it on shallow wedges (**3**). If it still doesn't fit take it down and remove more wood where appropriate.

1 Saw off horns

2 Plane to size

3 Wedge the door

Fitting hinges

The upper hinge is set about 175mm (7in) from the door's top edge and the lower one about 250mm (10in) from the bottom. They are cut equally into the stile and door frame. Wedge the door in its opening and, with the wedges tapped in to raise it to the right floor clearance, mark the positions of the hinges on both the door and frame.

Stand the door on edge, the hinge stile uppermost, open a hinge and, with its knuckle projecting from the edge of the door, align it with the marks and draw round the flap with a pencil (**1**). Set a marking gauge (◁) to the thickness of the flap and mark the depth of the housing. With a chisel make a series of shallow cuts across the grain (**2**) and pare out the waste to the scored line. Repeat the procedure with the second hinge, then, using the flaps as guides, drill pilot holes for the screws and fix both hinges into their housings.

Wedge the door in the open position, aligning the free hinge flaps with the marks on the door frame. Make sure that the knuckles of the hinges are parallel with the frame, then trace the housings on the frame (**3**) and cut them out as you did the others.

Adjusting and aligning

Hang the door with one screw holding each hinge and see if it closes smoothly. If the latch stile rubs on the frame you may have to make one or both housings slightly deeper. If the door strains against the hinges it is what is called 'hinge bound'. In this case insert thin cardboard beneath the hinge flaps to pack them out. When the door finally opens and closes properly drive in the rest of the screws.

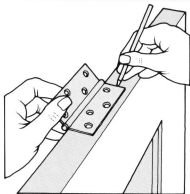

1 Mark round the flap with a pencil

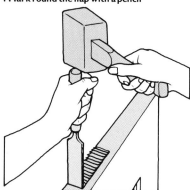

2 Cut across the grain with a chisel

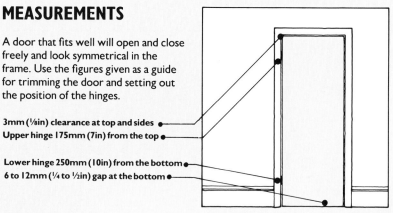

3 Mark the size of the flap on the frame

MEASUREMENTS

A door that fits well will open and close freely and look symmetrical in the frame. Use the figures given as a guide for trimming the door and setting out the position of the hinges.

3mm (1/8in) clearance at top and sides •

Upper hinge 175mm (7in) from the top •

Lower hinge 250mm (10in) from the bottom •

6 to 12mm (1/4 to 1/2in) gap at the bottom •

Rising butt hinges

Rising butt hinges lift a door as it is opened and are fitted to prevent it dragging on thick pile carpet.

They are made in two parts: a flap, with a fixed pin, which is screwed to the door frame, and another, with a single knuckle, which is fixed to the door, the knuckle sliding over the pin.

Rising butt hinges can be fixed only one way up, and are therefore made specifically for left- or right-hand opening. The countersunk screwholes in the fixed pin flap indicate the side to which it is made to be fitted.

Fitting

Trim the door and mark the hinge positions (See opposite), but before fitting the hinges plane a shallow bevel at the top outer corner of the hinge stile so that it will clear the frame as it opens. As the stile (▷) runs through to the top of the door, plane from the outer corner towards the centre to avoid splitting the wood. The top strip of the door stop will mask the bevel when the door is closed.

Fit the hinges to the door and the frame, then lower the door on to the hinge pins, taking care not to damage the architrave above the opening.

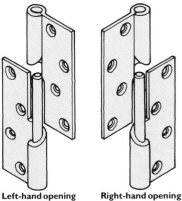

Left-hand opening   Right-hand opening

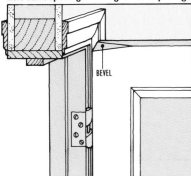

BEVEL

Plane a shallow bevel to clear the door frame

Weatherproofing a door

Fitting a weatherboard

A weatherboard is a special moulding fitted to the bottom of an outer door to shed rainwater away from the threshold. To fit one measure the width of the opening between the door stops and cut the moulding to fit, cutting one end at a slight angle where it meets the door frame on the latch side. This will allow it to clear the frame as the door swings open.

Make a weatherproof seal between the moulding and the door. On an unfinished door use screws and a waterproof adhesive to attach the moulding. On a pre-painted one apply a thick coat of primer to the back surface of the moulding and screw it into place while the primer is still wet. Fill or plug all screwholes and thoroughly prime and finish the surfaces.

Allowing for a weather bar

Though a rebate cut into the head and side posts of an outer door frame provides a seal round an inward opening door, a rebate cut into the sill at the foot of the door would merely encourage water to flow into the house.

Unless protected by a porch, a door in an exposed position needs to be fitted with a weather bar to prevent rainwater running underneath.

This is a metal or plastic strip which is set into the step or sill. If you are putting in a new door and wish to fit a weather bar, use a router or power saw to cut a rebate across the bottom of the door in order to clear the bar.

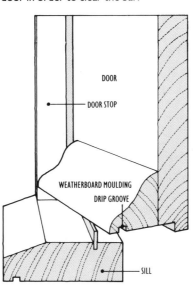

DOOR

DOOR STOP

WEATHERBOARD MOULDING

DRIP GROOVE

SILL

Door fitted with a weather board

ADJUSTING BUTT HINGES

Perhaps you have a door catching on a bump in the floor as it opens. You can, of course, fit rising butt hinges, but the problem can be overcome by resetting the lower hinge so that its knuckle projects slightly more than the top one. The door will still hang vertically when closed, but as it opens the out-of-line pins will throw it upwards so that the bottom edge will clear the bump.

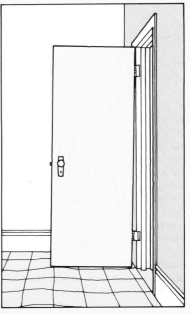

Resetting the hinge
You may have to reset both hinges to the new angle to prevent binding.

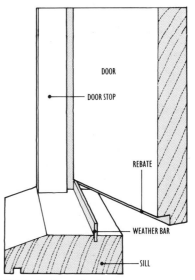

DOOR

DOOR STOP

REBATE

WEATHER BAR

SILL

Sill fitted with weather bar

FIXING A DOOR CASING

A new internal door opening will need a casing to finish it. These are usually of board 25mm (1in) thick where the applied door stop is used, or 38mm (1½in) when they are rebated to take the door. The width of the casing should equal the thickness of the finished wall.

Door casings are available from joinery suppliers in unassembled kits for standard door sizes. If your door is not standard you can make a lining, using a bare faced tongue-and-groove joint (1).

Wedge the assembled and braced frame in position in the opening (2) and place hardboard or plywood packing between the lintel and the soffit casing at each end if necessary. Check that the edges project equally from both faces of the wall and nail the soffit casing with two 75mm (3in) oval or cut clasp nails.

Plumb one jamb casing with a straight edge and spirit level and pack it in place (3). Start nailing about 75mm (3in) from the bottom and work up, checking the casing for true as you go. Place the nails in pairs 450mm (1ft 6in) apart.

Cut a 'pinch rod' to fit closely between the jamb casings at the top of the frame, then place it across the bottom and pack out the unfixed jamb to fit (4). Check that the jamb is plumb. Nail the casing in place and use the pinch rod to check the distance between the jamb casings at all levels.

Finish the wall surface round the opening and cover the joint with a mitred architrave moulding.

Hang the door and fit the door stop battens to the inside of the casing.

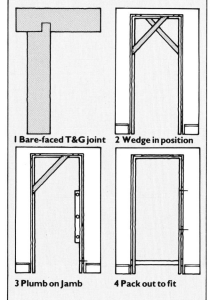

1 Bare-faced T&G joint   2 Wedge in position

3 Plumb on Jamb   4 Pack out to fit

RENEWING A DOOR FRAME

External door frames are built into the brickwork as it is erected, so replacing an old one means some damage to the plaster or the outside rendering.

In older houses the frames are recessed into the brickwork, the inside face of the frame flush with the plaster work and the architrave covering the joint. Modern houses may have frames close to or flush with the outer face of the brickwork. Work from the side the frame is closest to.

Measure the door and buy a standard frame to fit, or make one from standard frame sections.

Removing the old frame

Chop back the plaster or rendering with a chisel to expose the back face of the door frame (1).

With a general-purpose saw (2) cut through the three metal fixings holding the frame in the brickwork on each side, two about 225mm (9in) from the top and bottom and one half-way up.

Saw through the jambs half way up (3), and if necessary cut the head member and the sill. Lever the frame members out with a crowbar.

Clear any loose material from the opening and repair a vertical DPC in a cavity wall with gun-applied mastic to keep moisture out of the gap between inner and outer layers of brickwork.

Fitting the new frame

Fitting a frame is easier with its horns removed, but this weakens it. If possible fit the frame with horns shaped like the old ones (See right).

Wedge the frame in position, checking that it is central, square and plumb. Drill three counterbored clearance holes in each jamb for the fixing screws, positioned about 300mm (1ft) from the top and bottom with one half way, but avoid drilling in mortar joints. Run a masonry drill through the clearance holes to mark their position on the brickwork.

Remove the frame, drill the holes in the brickwork and insert No 12 wall plugs. Replace the frame and fix it with 100mm (4in) No 12 steel screws. Plug the counterbores.

Pack any gap under the sill with mortar. Make good the brickwork, rendering or plasterwork and apply mastic sealant round the outer edge of the frame to seal any small gaps. Fit the door as described (◁).

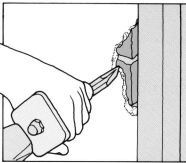

1 Cut back to expose the back of the frame

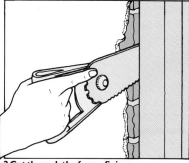

2 Cut through the frame fixings

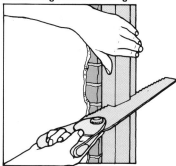

3 Saw through the frame to remove it

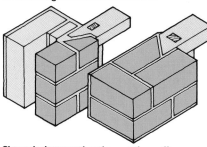

Shape the horns rather than cut them off

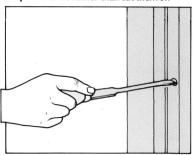

Screw the frame to the plugged wall

REPAIRING A ROTTEN FRAME

The great majority of external door frames are constructed of softwood, and this, if it is regularly maintained with a good paint system, will give years of excellent service. However, the ends of door sills and the frame posts are vulnerable to wet rot if they are subject to continual wetting. This can happen when the frame has moved because of shrinkage of the timber, or where old pointing has fallen out and left a gap where water can get in. Alternatively, old and porous brickwork or an ineffective damp-proof course can be the cause of wet-rot damage.

Prevention is always better than any cure, so check round the frame for any shrinkage gaps and apply a mastic sealant where necessary. Keep all pointing in good order. A slight outbreak of rot can be treated with the aid of a proprietary repair kit and preservative.

It is possible for the sill to rot without the frame posts being affected. In this case just replace the sill. If the posts are also affected, repair them (See right). In some cases the post ends can be tenoned into the sill and fitted as a unit.

Replacing a sill

You can buy 150 x 50mm (6 x 2in) softwood or hardwood door sill sections which can be cut to the required length. If your sill is not of a standard-shaped section the replacement can be made to order. It is more economical in the longer run to specify a hardwood such as oak or utile, as it will last much longer.

Taking out the old
First measure and note down the width of the door opening, then remove the door. The posts are usually tenoned into the sill, so to separate the sill from them split it lengthwise with a wood chisel. A saw cut across the centre of the sill can make the job easier.

The ends of the sill are set into the brickwork on either side, so cut away the bricks to make the removal of the old sill and insertion of the new one easier. Use a plugging chisel to cut carefully through the mortar round the bricks and try to preserve them for reuse after fitting the sill.

The new sill has to be inserted from the front so that it can be tucked under the posts and into the brickwork. Cut the tenons off level with the shoulders of the posts (1). Mark and cut shallow housings for the ends of the posts in the top of the new sill, spaced apart as previously noted. The housings must be deep enough to take the full width of the posts (2), which may mean the sill being slightly higher than the original one, so that you will have to trim a little off the bottom of the door.

Fitting the new
Try the new sill for fit and check that it is level. Before fixing it apply a wood preservative to its underside and ends, and, as a measure against rising or penetrating damp, apply two or three coats of bitumen latex emulsion to the brickwork.

When both treatments are dry, glue the sill to the posts, using an exterior woodworking adhesive. Wedge the underside of the sill with slate to push it up against the ends of the posts, skew-nail the posts to it and leave it for the adhesive to set.

Pack the gap between the underside of the sill and the masonry with a stiff mortar of 3 parts sand: 1 part cement, and rebond and point the bricks. Finish by treating the wood with preservative and applying a mastic sealant round the door frame.

1 Cut tenons off level with the joint's shoulder

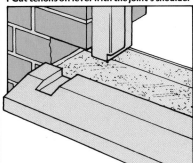

2 Cut a housing to receive the post

REPAIRING DOOR POSTS

Rot can attack the ends of door posts, particularly in exposed positions where they meet stone steps or are set into concrete, as is found in some garages. The posts may be located on metal dowels set into the step.

If the damage is not too extensive the rotten end can be cut away and replaced with a new piece, either scarf jointed or half lap jointed into place. If your situation involves a wooden sill combine the following information with that given for replacing a sill (See left).

First remove the door, then saw off the end of the affected post back to sound timber. For a scarf joint make the cut at 45 degrees to the face of the post (1). For a lap joint cut it square. Chip any metal dowel out of the step with a cold chisel.

Measure and cut a matching section of post to the required length, allowing for the overlap of the joint, then cut the end to 45 degrees or mark and cut a half lap joint in both parts of the post (2).

Drill a hole in the end of the new section for the metal dowel if it is still usable. If it is not, make a new one from a piece of galvanized steel gas pipe, priming the metal to prevent corrosion. Treat the new wood with a chemical preservative and insert the dowel. Set the dowel in mortar, at the same time gluing and screwing the joint (3).

If a dowel is not used, fix the post to the wall with counterbored screws. Place hardboard or plywood packing behind it if necessary and plug the counterbores of the screw holes.

Apply a mastic sealant to the joints between the door post, wall and base.

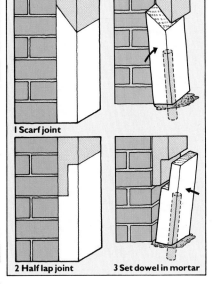

1 Scarf joint

2 Half lap joint   **3 Set dowel in mortar**

SEE ALSO

Details for: ▷
Door frames   61

WINDOWS: TYPES AND CONSTRUCTION

SEE ALSO

◁ Details for:
Repairing windows 69–73

The function of any window is to allow natural light into the house and to provide ventilation. Traditionally windows have been referred to as 'lights', and the term 'fixed light' is still used to describe a window or part of a window frame that doesn't open. A section that opens for ventilation, the 'sash', is a separate frame that slides vertically or is hinged at its side, top or bottom edge. Windows of the hinged type are commonly referred to as casement windows.

A pane of glass can also be pivoted horizontally as a single sash, or several panes can be grouped together to make up a louvre window.

Most window frames and sashes are made up from moulded sections of solid wood. Mild steel and, more recently, aluminium or rigid plastic are also used, though frames of these materials are usually fixed to the brickwork by means of wooden sub-frames.

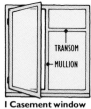

I Casement window

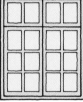

2 Glazing-bars

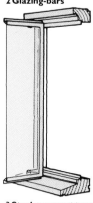

3 Steel casement type

Casement windows

Window frames with hinged sashes – casement windows – are the most common and are now produced in the widest range of materials and styles.

A traditional wooden window frame and its hinged sash are constructed in much the same way as a door and its frame. A jamb at each side is mortice-and-tenon jointed into the head member at the top and into a sill at the bottom (See below). The frame may be divided vertically by a 'mullion', or horizontally by a 'transom' (I).

The sash, which is carried by the frame, has its top and bottom rails jointed into its side stiles. Glazing bars, relatively light moulded sections, are used to sub-divide the glazed area for smaller panes (2).

Side-hung sashes are fitted on butt hinges or sometimes, for better access to the outside of the glass, on 'easy clean' extension hinges. A lever fastener, or 'cockspur', for securing the sash is screwed to the middle of the stile on the opening side. A casement stay on the bottom rail holds the sash in various open positions and acts as a locking device when the sash is closed. Top-hung sashes, or vents, are secured with a stay only.

Galvanized mild steel casement windows (3) were once popular for domestic use. They are made in the same format as wooden hinged windows but have a slimmer framework. The joints of the metal sections are welded.

Mild steel windows are strong and long-lasting but vulnerable to rust unless protected by galvanized plating or a good paint system. The rusting can be caused by weathering outside or by condensation on the inside.

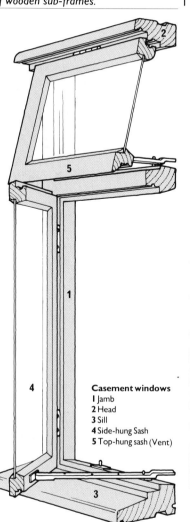

Casement windows
I Jamb
2 Head
3 Sill
4 Side-hung Sash
5 Top-hung sash (Vent)

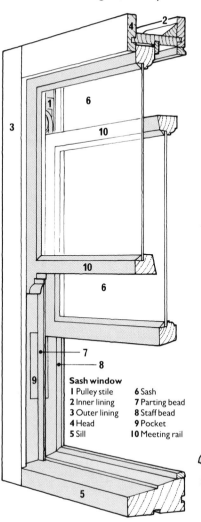

Sash window
I Pulley stile
2 Inner lining
3 Outer lining
4 Head
5 Sill
6 Sash
7 Parting bead
8 Staff bead
9 Pocket
10 Meeting rail

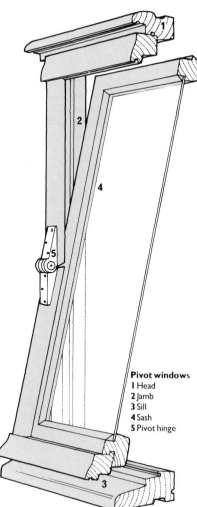

Pivot windows
I Head
2 Jamb
3 Sill
4 Sash
5 Pivot hinge

WINDOWS: TYPES AND CONSTRUCTION

Sash windows

Vertically sliding windows are commonly known as sash windows and when both top and bottom sashes can be opened they are referred to as 'double hung' sash windows.

The traditional wooden type (See opposite) is constructed with a 'box frame' in which the jambs are made up from three boards: the pulley stile, the inner lining and the outer lining. A back completes the box that houses the sash counterweights. The head is made up in a similar way but without the back lining, and the sill is of solid wood. The pulley stiles are jointed into the sill and the linings are set in a rebate.

The sashes of a double hung window are held in tracks formed by the outer lining, a parting bead and an inner staff bead. The beads can be removed for servicing the sash mechanism. Each sash is counterbalanced by two cast-iron weights – one at each side – which are attached by strong cords or chains that pass over pulleys in the stiles. Access to the weights is through 'pockets' – removable pieces of wood – set in the lower part of the stiles.

The top sash slides in the outer track and overlaps the inner bottom sash at their horizontal 'meeting rails'. The closing faces of the meeting rails are bevelled, and their wedging action helps to prevent the sashes rattling. It also provides better clearance when the window is opened, and improves security when it is locked. The sashes are secured by two-part fasteners of various types fitted on the meeting rails.

Spiral balances

Modern wooden or aluminium vertically sliding sashes have spring-assisted spiral balances which do not need a deep box construction. Rather than being concealed, the slim balances are fitted on the faces of the stiles.

Spiral balances
The balances are usually fixed to the faces of the frame stiles and set in grooves in the sash stiles.

Pivot windows

Wooden-framed pivot windows (See opposite) are constructed in a similar way to casement windows, but the sash is held on a pair of strong pivot hinges which allow the window to be tilted right over for easy cleaning from inside. A safety roller arm can be fitted to the frame and set to prevent the window opening more than 115mm (4½in).

Pivoting roof windows are available for pitched roofs with slopes from 15 to 85 degrees. Like the standard pivoting windows, they can be fully reversed for cleaning. The windows are supplied double glazed with sealed units, and ventilators are incorporated in the frame or sash. The timbers are protected on the outside by a metal covering, and flashing kits are supplied for fitting to tile or slate roofs ($\triangleright$).

Louvre windows

A louvre window is another form of pivot window. The louvres are unframed 'blades' of glass, 4mm (5/32in) or 6mm (¼in) thick, which have their long edges ground and polished. The louvres are held at each end in light alloy carriers which pivot on an upright member, and this is screwed to a wooden frame. One side is fitted with an opening and locking mechanism which links all of the louvres so that they operate together as one.

Louvre windows are effective as ventilators but they do not provide good security. They are also difficult to draught-proof.

Where an opening is more than 1.07m (3ft 6in) in width two sets of louvres are best used, with the centre pair of uprights set back to back in order to form a mullion.

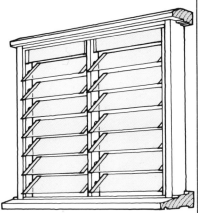

Use two sets of louvres for a wide opening

ALUMINIUM AND PLASTIC WINDOW FRAMES

Aluminium windows

These are now replacing old wooden and metal-framed windows. The aluminium is extruded into complex sections (1) to hold double-glazed sealed units and draught strips and – ready finished in white, satin silver, black or bronze – is maintenance free. These windows are highly engineered and complete with concealed projection hinges and lockable fasteners. They need no stays to hold them open.

To combat condensation the latest designs incorporate a 'thermal break' of insulating material in the hollow sections of the frame.

Most aluminium windows designed for replacement work are purpose-made and fitted by specialist companies. They need wooden sub-frames.

Plastic windows

Rigid plastic windows (2) are rather similar to aluminium ones but are thicker through their sections. They are manufactured in white plastic and once installed they require no maintenance.

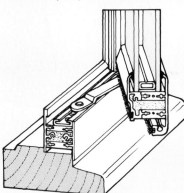

1 Extruded aluminium window set in wooden frame

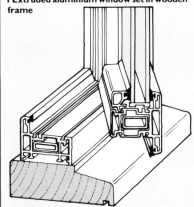

2 Metal tube-reinforced extruded-plastic window

HOW WINDOWS ARE FITTED

CONCRETE AND STEEL LINTELS

Solid walls

In older houses it is usual to find the window frame jambs set in recesses on the inside of the brickwork. The openings were formed before the windows were fitted and the frames were nailed or screwed into wooden plugs in the brickwork. No vertical damp-proof courses were fitted. Evaporation was relied on to keep the walls dry.

The frames in a 225mm (9in) thick wall were set flush with the inside. In a 340mm (1ft 1½in) wall they had inner reveals. All required sub-sills, usually stone ones, outside.

Brickwork above the opening in a traditional brick wall may be supported by a brick arch or a stone lintel. Flat or shallow curved arches were generally used, their thickness being the width of one brick. Wooden lintels were placed behind such arches to support the rest of the wall's thickness. Semi-circular arches were usually as thick as the wall.

Many stone lintels were carved to make decorative features. As with arches, an inner lintel shared the weight. Openings like this were never wide because of the relative weakness of the materials. The wide windows of main rooms had several openings divided by brick or stone columns.

Cavity walls

The window frames in modern houses are usually installed while the brickwork is being erected. They are fixed into place with metal brackets – 'frame cramps' – which are screwed to the frame's jambs and set in the mortar bed joints. There are three such cramps on each side of the frame.

Cavity walls must have a vertical damp-proof course. This is sandwiched between the brick outer leaf of the wall and the cavity-closing bricks of the inner leaf. The window frame is set forward in the opening and covers the joint. Some frames have the damp-proof courses fastened to them.

With the window frame in this position a good deal of the wall's thickness is exposed on the inside. The sides, or 'reveals' of the opening are finished off with plaster, as is the top, while the ledge at the bottom is finished with a window board which is tongued into a groove along the back of the frame sill.

The window board is also screwed or nailed down to the brickwork. Quarry tiles are sometimes used to form the inner sill.

Modern lintels are made from reinforced concrete or galvanized steel or a combination of both. These extremely strong lintels can support brickwork over a considerable span, enabling large picture windows to be installed without additional support.

A damp-proof course must be provided above the window opening to prevent any moisture in the cavity permeating the inner leaf and the window frame, though some metal lintels can be installed without additional damp-proof material.

The front face of a concrete 'through-the-wall' or 'boot' lintel can be seen above the opening. Where a brick facing is required a steel lintel is used and the bricks can be laid on the relatively thin metal edge in bonded courses or on their ends to simulate a brick arch.

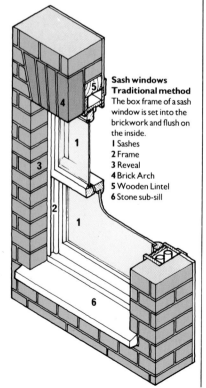

**Sash windows
Traditional method**
The box frame of a sash window is set into the brickwork and flush on the inside.
1 Sashes
2 Frame
3 Reveal
4 Brick Arch
5 Wooden Lintel
6 Stone sub-sill

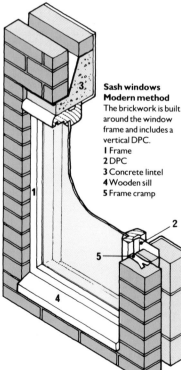

**Sash windows
Modern method**
The brickwork is built around the window frame and includes a vertical DPC.
1 Frame
2 DPC
3 Concrete lintel
4 Wooden sill
5 Frame cramp

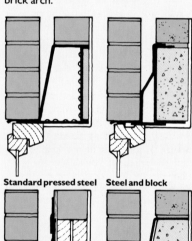
Standard pressed steel

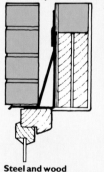
Steel and block

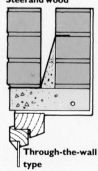
Steel and wood

Steel and concrete

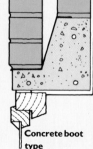

Through-the-wall type

Concrete boot type

REPAIRING ROTTEN FRAMES

Softwood is the traditional material for making wooden window frames, and providing it is of sound quality and is well cared for, it will last the life of the *building. New frames or frames which have been stripped should always be treated with a clear wood preservative before painting.*

Regular maintenance

It is the bottom rail of a softwood window frame that is most vulnerable to rot if it is not protected. The water may be absorbed by the wood through a poor paint finish or by penetrating behind old shrunken putty. An annual check of all window frames should be carried out and any faults should be dealt with. Old putty that has shrunk away from the glass should be cut out and replaced with new.

Remove old flaking paint, make good any cracks in the wood with a flexible filler and repaint, ensuring that the underside of the sash is well painted.

Replacing a sash rail

Where rot is well advanced and the rail is beyond repair it should be cut out and replaced. This should be done before the rot spreads to the stiles of the frame. Otherwise you will eventually have to replace the whole sash frame.

Remove the sash either by unscrewing the hinges or – if it is a double-hung sash window – by removing the beading (▷).

With a little care the repair can be carried out without the glass being removed from the sash frame, though if the window is large it would be safer to take out the glass. In any event, cut away the putty from the damaged rail.

The bottom rail is tenoned into the stiles (1), but it can be replaced by using bridle joints. Saw down the shoulder lines of the tenon joints (2) from both faces of the frame and remove the rail.

Make a new rail, or buy a piece if it is a standard section, and mark and cut it to length with a full-width tenon at each end. Set the positions of the tenons to line up with the mortises of the stiles. Cut the shoulders to match the rebated sections of the stiles (3) or, if it has a decorative moulding, pare the moulding away to leave a flat shoulder (4).

Cut slots in the ends of the stiles to receive the tenons.

Glue the new rail into place with a waterproof resin adhesive and reinforce the two joints with pairs of 6mm (1/4in) stopped dowels. Drill the stopped holes from the inside of the sash frame and stagger them.

When the adhesive is dry, plane the surface as required and treat the new wood with a clear preservative. Re-putty the glass and paint the new rail within three weeks.

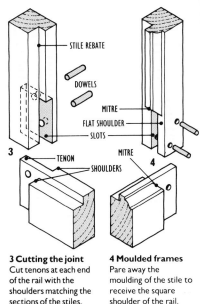

1 The original joint
The rail is tenoned into the stile and fitted with wedges.

2 Cutting out the rail
Saw down the shoulder lines of the joints from both faces of the frame.

3 Cutting the joint
Cut tenons at each end of the rail with the shoulders matching the sections of the stiles.

4 Moulded frames
Pare away the moulding of the stile to receive the square shoulder of the rail. Mitre the moulding.

REPLACING A FIXED-LIGHT RAIL

The frames of some fixed lights are made like sashes but are screwed to the main frame jamb and mullion. Such a frame can be repaired in the same way as a sash (See left) after its glass is removed and it is unscrewed from the window frame. Where this proves too difficult you will have to carry out the repair in situ.

First remove the putty and the glass, then saw through the rail at each end. With a chisel trim the rebated edge of the jamb(s) and/or mullion to a clean surface at the joint (1) and chop out the old tenons. Cut a new length of rail to fit between the prepared edges and cut housings in its top edge at both ends to take loose tenons. Place the housings so that they line up with the mortises and make them twice as long as the depth of the mortises.

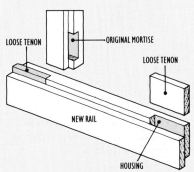

1 Chop out the tenons and cut a new rail to fit

Cut two loose tenons to fit the housings, and two packing pieces. The latter should have one sloping edge (2).

Apply an exterior woodworking adhesive to all of the jointing surfaces, place the rail between the frame members, insert the loose tenons and push them sideways into the mortises. Drive the packing pieces behind the tenons to lock them in place. When the adhesive has set, trim the top edges, treat the new wood with clear preservative, replace the glass and re-putty. Paint within three weeks.

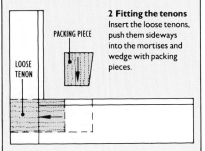

2 Fitting the tenons
Insert the loose tenons, push them sideways into the mortises and wedge with packing pieces.

SEE ALSO

Details for: ▷
Removing beading | 71

● **Removing glass**
Removing glass from a window frame in one piece is not easy so be prepared for it to break. Apply adhesive tape across the glass to bind the pieces together if it should break. Chisel away the putty to leave a clean rebate, then pull out the sprigs (▷). Work the blade of a putty knife into the bedding joint on the inside of the frame to break the grip of the putty. Steady the glass and lift it out when it becomes free.

REPAIRING ROTTEN SILLS

The sill is a fundamental part of a window frame, and one attacked by rot can mean major repair work.

A casement window frame is constructed in the same way as a door frame and can be repaired in a similar way (◁). All the glass should be removed first. The window board may also have to be removed, then refitted level with the replacement sill.

Make sure that the damp-proofing of the joint between the underside of the sill and the wall is maintained. Modern gun-applied mastics have made this particular problem easier to overcome. Some traditional frames have a galvanized-iron water bar between the sill and sub-sill. When replacing a sill of this type without removing the whole frame it may be necessary to remove the bar and rely on mastic sealants alone to keep the water out.

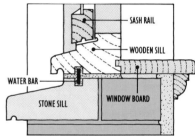

Traditional frame with stone sub-sill

Replacing a wooden sill

If you simply replace a sill by cutting through it and fitting a new section between the jambs you may not have solved your problem. Even when mastic sealants are used, any breakdown of the seal will allow water a direct path to the brickwork and the end grain of the wood, and you may find yourself doing the job all over again.

Serious rot in the sill of a sash window may require the whole frame to be taken out (◁). Make and fit a new sill using the old one as a pattern. Treat the new wood with a preservative and take the opportunity to treat the old wood which is normally hidden by the brickwork. Apply a bead of mastic sealant to the sill, then replace the complete frame in the opening from inside. Make good the plaster.

It is possible to replace the sill from the inside with the frame in place. Saw through the sill close to the jambs and remove the cut centre portion. Cut away the bottom ends of the inner lining level with the pulley stiles and remove the ends of the old sill. Cut the ends of the new sill to fit round the outer lining and under the stiles and inner lining. Fit the sill and nail or screw the stiles to it.

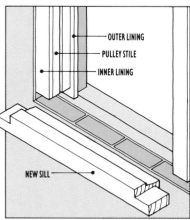

Cut the new sill to fit the frame

Repairing a stone sub-sill

The traditional stone sills that feature in older houses may become eroded by the weather if they are not protected with paint. They may also suffer cracking due to subsidence in part of the wall.

Repair any cracks and eroded surfaces with a quick-setting waterproof cement. Rake the cracks out to clean and enlarge them, then dampen the stone with clean water and work the cement well into the cracks, finishing off flush with the top surface.

Depressions caused by erosion should be undercut to provide the cement with a good hold. A thin layer of cement simply applied to a shallow depression in the surface will not last. Use a cold chisel to cut away the surface of the sill at least 25mm (1in) below the finished level and remove all traces of dust.

Make a wooden former to the shape of the sill and temporarily nail it to the brickwork. Dampen the stone, pour in the cement and tamp it level with the former, then smooth it with a trowel. Leave it to set for a couple of days before removing the former. Let it dry thoroughly before painting.

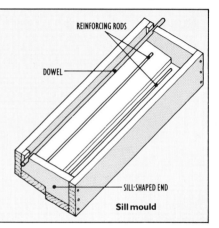

Make a wooden former to the shape of the sill

CASTING A NEW SUB-SILL

Cut out the remains of the old stone sill with a hammer and cold chisel. Make a wooden mould with its end pieces shaped to the same section as the old sill. The mould must be made upside down, its open top representing the underside of the sill.

Fill two thirds of the mould with fine ballast concrete, tamped down well, and then add two lengths of mild steel reinforcing rod, judiciously spaced to share the volume of the sill, then fill the remainder of the mould. Set a narrow piece of wood such as a dowel into notches previously cut in the ends of the mould. This is to form a 'throat' or drip groove in the underside of the sill.

Cover the concrete with polythene sheeting or dampen it regularly for two or three days to prevent rapid drying. When the concrete is set (allow about seven days) remove it from the mould and re-lay the sill in the wall on a bed of mortar to meet the wooden sill.

Sill mould

RE-CORDING A SASH WINDOW

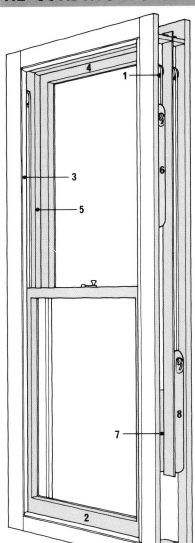

The workings of a double-hung sash window

1 Pulleys	**5** Parting bead
2 Bottom sash	**6** Bottom sash weight
3 Staff bead	**7** Pocket
4 Top sash	**8** Top sash weight

The sash cording from which the sashes are suspended will wear and in time will break. You should replace both cords even when only one has broken.

Waxed sash cording is normally sold in standard hanks, though some suppliers sell it by the metre. Each sash will require two lengths about three quarters the height of the window. Do not cut it to length beforehand.

Removing the sashes

Lower the sashes and cut through the cords with a knife to release the weights. Hold on to the cords and lower the weights as far as possible before letting them drop. Prise off the side staff beads from inside the frame, starting in the middle and bowing them to make their mitred ends spring out and avoid breakage.

Lean the inner sash forward and mark the ends of the cord grooves on the face of the sash stiles. Reposition the sash and carry the marks on to the pulley stiles (**1**). The sash can now be pulled clear of the frame.

Carefully prise out the two parting beads from their grooves in the stiles. The top sash can then be removed, after marking the ends of the grooves as before. Place sashes safely aside.

To gain access to the weights take out the pocket pieces which were trapped by the parting bead and lift the weights out through the openings. Hanging pieces of thin wood known as parting strips may be fitted inside the box stiles to keep the pairs of weights apart. Push these aside to reach the outer weights.

Remove the old cording from the weights and sashes and clean them up ready for the new sash cords.

Fitting the sashes

The top sash is fitted first, but not before all of the sash cords and weights are in place. Clean away any build-up of paint from the pulleys. Tie a length of fine string to one end of the sash cord. Weight the other end of the string with small nuts or a piece of chain. Thread the weight – known as a mouse – over a pulley (**2**) and pull the string through the pocket opening until the cord is pulled through. Attach the end of the cord to a weight with a special knot (See below left).

Use the sash marks to measure the length of cord required. Pull on the cord to hoist the weight up to the pulley. Then let it drop back about 100mm (4in). Hold it temporarily in this position with a nail driven into the stile just below the pulley. Cut the cord level with the mark on the pulley stile (**3**).

Repeat this procedure for the cord on the other side, and then for the bottom sash.

Replace the top sash on the sill, removing the temporary nails in turn. Lean the sash forward, locate the cords into the grooves in the stiles and nail them in place using three or four 25mm (1in) round wire nails. Nail only the bottom 150mm (6in), not all the way up (**4**). Lift the sash to check that the weights do not touch bottom.

Replace the pocket pieces and pin the parting beads in their grooves. Fit the bottom sash in the same way. Finally replace the staff beads; take care to position them accurately.

SEE ALSO

Details for: ▷
Sash window   66

HOW TO TIE A SASH WEIGHT KNOT

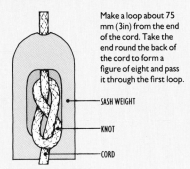

Make a loop about 75 mm (3in) from the end of the cord. Take the end round the back of the cord to form a figure of eight and pass it through the first loop.

SASH WEIGHT

KNOT

CORD

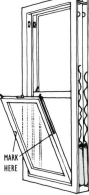

1 Mark cord grooves

MARK HERE

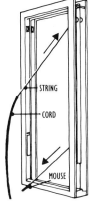

2 Pull cord through

STRING

CORD

MOUSE

3 Cut cords at mark

CUT HERE

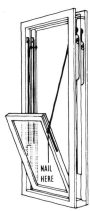

4 Nail cord to sash

NAIL HERE

SPIRAL BALANCES

Instead of cords and counterweights, modern sash windows use spiral balances which are mounted on the faces of the frame stiles, eliminating the need for traditional box sections. The balances are made to order to match the size and weight of individual glazed sashes and can be ordered through builders' merchants or by post from the makers using an order form.

Spiral balance components

Each balance consists of a torsion spring and a spiral rod housed in a tube. The top end is fixed to the stile and the inner spiral to the bottom of the sash. The complete unit can be housed in a groove in the sash stile or in the jamb of the frame.

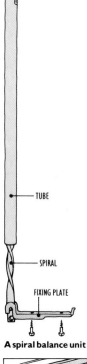

TUBE

SPIRAL

FIXING PLATE

A spiral balance unit

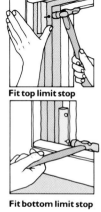

Fit top limit stop

Fit bottom limit stop

Fitting the balances

You can fit spiral sash balances to replace the weights in a traditionally constructed sash window.

Remove the sashes and weigh them on your bathroom scales. Place your order, giving the weight of each sash and its height and width, also the height of the frame. Refit the sashes temporarily until the balances arrive, then take them out again and remove the pulleys.

Plug the holes and paint the stiles. Cut grooves, as specified by the manufacturers, in the stiles of each sash, to take the balances (**1**). Also cut a housing at each end of their bottom edges to receive the spiral rod fixing plates. Fit the plates with screws (**2**).

Sit the top sash in place, resting it on the sill, and fit the parting bead. Take the top pair of balances, which are shorter than those for the bottom sash, and locate each in its groove (**3**). Fix the top ends of the balance tubes to the frame stiles with the screw nails provided (**4**) and set the ends tight against the head.

Lift the sash to its full height and prop it with a length of wood. Hook the wire 'key', provided by the makers, into the hole in the end of each spiral rod and pull each one down about 150mm (6in). Keeping the tension on the spring, add three to five turns anti-clockwise (**5**). Locate the ends of the rods in the fixing plate and test the balance of the sash. If it drops add another turn on the springs until it is just held in position. Take care not to overwind the balances.

Fit the bottom sash in the same way, refitting the staff bead to hold it in place. Fit the stops that limit the full travel of the sashes in their respective tracks (See left).

RENOVATING SPIRAL BALANCES

In time the springs of spiral balances may weaken. Re-tension them by unhooking the spiral rods from the fixing plates, then turning the rods anti-clockwise once or twice.

The mechanisms can be serviced by releasing the tension and unwinding the rods from the tubes. Wipe them clean and apply a little thin oil, then rewind the rods back into the tubes and tension them as described above.

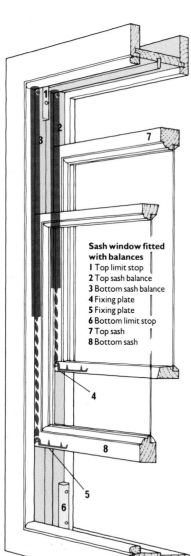

Sash window fitted with balances
1 Top limit stop
2 Top sash balance
3 Bottom sash balance
4 Fixing plate
5 Fixing plate
6 Bottom limit stop
7 Top sash
8 Bottom sash

1 Cut a groove in the sash stiles

2 Fix the plates in their housings with screws

3 Fit the sash and locate the tube in its groove

4 Nail the top end of the tube to the stile

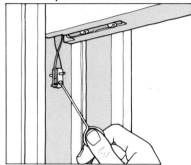

5 Tension the springs with the key provided

READY-MADE WINDOWS

Joinery suppliers offer a range of ready-made window frames in both hardwood and softwood, and some typical examples are shown below.

Unfortunately the range of sizes is rather limited, but where a ready-made frame is fairly close to one's requirements it is possible to either cut back the brickwork or fill the gap between the frame and the wall with masonry, though this is really acceptable only for windows in rendered walls. In a wall of exposed brickwork the window frame should be made to measure.

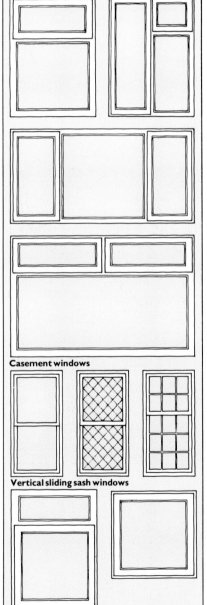

Casement windows

Vertical sliding sash windows

Pivot windows

REPLACEMENT WINDOWS

The style of the windows is an important element in the appearance of any house. Should you be thinking of replacing windows in an older dwelling you might find it better – and not necessarily more expensive – to have new wooden frames made rather than changing to modern windows of aluminium or plastic.

Planning and building regulations

Window conversions do not normally need planning permission as they come under the heading of house improvement or home maintenance, but if you plan to alter your windows significantly – for example, by bricking one up or making a new window opening, or both – you should consult your local Building Control Officer.

All authorities require minimum levels of ventilation to be provided in the habitable rooms of a house, and this normally means that the openable part of windows must have an area at least one twentieth that of the room.

You should also check with your local authority if you live in a listed building or in a conservation area, which could mean some limitation on your choice.

Buying replacement windows

Specialist joinery firms will make up wooden window frames to your size. Specify hardwood or, for a painted finish, softwood impregnated with a timber preservative.

Alternatively you can approach one of the replacement window companies, though this is likely to limit your choice to aluminium or plastic frames. The ready-glazed units can be fitted to your old timber sub-frames or to new hardwood ones supplied by the installer. Most of the replacement window companies operate on the basis of supplying and also fitting the windows, and their service includes disposing of the old windows and of the rubbish.

This method is saving of time and labour, but you should carefully compare the various offerings of these companies and their compatibility with the style of your house before opting for one. Choose a frame that reproduces, as closely as possible, the proportions of the original window.

Replacing a casement window

Measure the width and height of the window opening. If the replacement window will need a timber sub-frame and the existing one is in good condition, take your measurements from inside the frame. Otherwise take them from the brickwork. You may have to cut away some of the rendering or plaster first so as to get accurate measurements. Order the replacement window accordingly.

Remove the old window by first taking out the sashes and then the panes of glass in any fixed part. Unscrew the exposed fixings, such as may be found in a metal frame, or chisel away the plaster or rendering and cut through them with a hacksaw. It should be possible to knock the frame out in one piece, but if not saw through it in several places and lever the pieces out with a crowbar **(1)** . Clean up the exposed brickwork with a bolster chisel to make a neat opening.

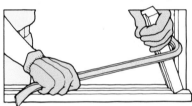

1 Lever out the pieces of the old frame

Cut the horns off the new frame if present, then plumb the frame in the window opening and wedge it **(2)** . Drill screw holes through the stiles into the brickwork **(3)** , then remove the frame and plug the holes. Attach a bituminous felt damp-proof course to the stiles and sill and refit the frame, checking again that it is plumb before screwing it into home.

Make good the wall with mortar and plaster. Gaps of 6mm (¼in) or less can be filled with mastic. Glaze the new frame as required.

2 Fit the new frame   **3 Drill fixing holes**

REPLACEMENT WINDOWS

Bay windows

A bay window is a combination of window frames which are built out from the face of the building. The side frames may be set at 90, 60 or 45 degree angles to the front of the house. Curved bays are also made with equal-sized frames set at a very slight angle to each other to form a faceted curve.

The frames of a bay window are set on brickwork which is built to the shape of the bay, which may be at ground level only, with a flat or pitched roof, or may be continued up through all storeys and finished with a gabled roof.

Bay windows can break away from the main wall through subsidence caused by poor foundations or differential ground movements. Damage from slight movement can be repaired once it has stabilised. Repoint the brickwork and apply mastic sealant to gaps round the woodwork. Damage from extensive or persistent movement should be dealt with by a builder. Consult your local Building Control Officer and inform your house insurance company.

Fitting the frame

Where the height of the original window permits it, standard window frames can be used to make up a replacement bay window. Using gasket seals (See left), various combinations of frames can be arranged. Shaped hardwood corner posts are available to give a 90, 60 or 45 degree angle to the side frames. The gasket is used for providing a weatherproof seal between the posts and the frames.

Joining frames
A flexible gasket, which is sold by the metre, is available for joining standard frames. The frames are screwed together to fit the opening.

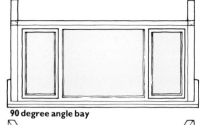
90 degree angle bay

60 degree angle bay

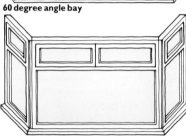
45 degree angle bay

Hardwood bay window (Detail)

Bow windows

These are windows constructed on a shallow curve, and they normally project from a flat wall. Complete hardwood bow window frames are available from joinery suppliers, ready for installation in a brickwork opening. A flat-topped canopy of moulded plastic is made for finishing the top of the window. Bow windows can be substituted for conventional ones.

Fitting the frame

Tack a damp-proof course material to the sides of the frame and the underside of the sill, then fit the frame and the canopy into the wall opening together, the outer edges of the frame set flush with the wall finish. Screw the frame to the brickwork. The vertical damp-proofing should overlap the one in the wall if one is present.

Weatherproof the canopy with a lead flashing cut into the wall and dressed over the canopy upstand. Use mastic to seal the joints between the frame's sides and sill and the brickwork.

Bow window (Detail) with leaded lights

REPLACING A SASH WINDOW

An old vertically sliding sash window with cords and counterweights can be replaced with a new frame fitted with spiral balance sashes.

Remove the sashes (◁), then take out the old frame from inside the room. Prise off the architrave, then the window boards, and chop away the plaster as necessary. Most frames make a wedge fit, and you can loosen one by hitting the sill on the outside with a heavy hammer and a wood block. Lift the frame out of the opening when it is loose (1) and remove any debris from the opening once it is clear.

Set the new frame centrally in the opening so that its stiles are showing equal amounts on each side of the exterior brickwork reveals. Check the frame for plumb and wedge the corners at the head and the sill. Make up the space left by the old box stiles with mortared brickwork (2).

Metal brackets screwed to the frame's stiles can also be set in the mortar bed joints to secure the frame.

When the mortar is set, replaster the inner wall and replace the architrave. In the meantime glaze the sashes. Finally apply a mastic sealant to the joints between the outside brickwork and the frame to keep the weather out.

1 Lift out old frame   **2 Fill gaps with brick**

ROOF WINDOWS

Double-glazed roof windows are becoming increasingly popular for the modernizing of old attic skylights and as part of loft conversions. They are supplied ready-glazed and fully-equipped with catches and ventilators. Flashing kits to fit the window frame and to suit high or low profile roofing materials are also available.

Centre-pivoting sashes can be used on roofs with pitches between 15 and 85 degrees, and special emergency exit types may be installed. These can be converted to top-hung or side-hung sashes at the turn of a handle. The former are for roof pitches of 20-60 degrees, and the latter for those of 60-85 degrees.

Roof windows are relatively easy to install using only ordinary woodworking tools and often working only from the inside. Once they are fitted the glass can be cleaned comfortably from the inside. Such accessories as blinds and remote opening devices are also available.

Roof windows reverse for easy maintenance

Blinds which fit the inside frame are available

Choosing the size

The manufacturers of roof windows offer a standard range of sizes and, apart from consideration of cost, the overall size should take account of the area of glass necessary to provide a suitable level of daylight in the room.

The height of the window is also quite important. It should be determined by the pitch of the roof in relation to how the window is going to be used. The manufacturers produce charts which give the recommended dimensions according to roof pitch. Ideally, if the window is to provide a good outlook, the bottom rails should not obstruct the view at normal seat height, nor should it cut across the line of sight of someone standing. Broadly this means that the shallower the pitch of the roof, the taller the window needs to be. The top of the window should remain within comfortable reach.

Fitting a window

Start by stripping off the roof-covering material over the area which is to be occupied by the window. The final placing of the frame will be determined by the position of the rafters and the roofing. Start by setting the bottom of the window frame at the specified distance above the nearest full course of slates and try to position it so as to have half or whole slates at each side.

Cut through the slating battens, roofing felt and rafters to make the opening, following the dimensions given by the manufacturer. Cut and nail horizontal trimmers between the rafters to set the height of the opening, and a vertical trimmer or trimmers to set the width.

With the glazed sash removed, screw the window frame in place with the brackets provided. A guide line is clearly marked round the frame, and this must be set level with the surface of the roofing battens. Check that the frame is square by measuring across its diagonals to be sure they are equal.

Complete the outside work by fitting the slates and flashing kit, working up from the bottom of the frame. Replace the glazed sash.

Cut and nail plasterboard to the sides of the rafters on the inside and close the top and bottom of the opening with plasterboard nailed in the groove provided in the frame and to the timbers of the roof structure.

Finish off the joints with filler and tape, ready for decoration (▷).

Standard-sized windows can be arranged side-by-side or one above the other to create a larger window. The widest single window available measures 1.34m (4ft 4¾in). When deciding on the size of a window bear in mind its proportions and its position in relation to the appearance of the building.

You will probably not need planning permission to install this type of window but check if you live in a listed building or in a conservation area. However, the structural alterations will have to have Building Regulations approval just as a complete loft conversion does.

The manufacturers of roof windows supply comprehensive fixing instructions to suit installation in all situations. Below is a summary of one type of window fitted into a slate-covered roof. The frame for a tiled roof has a different flashing kit.

SEE ALSO

Details for: ▷
Plasterboard   40–41

Height of window
The height should enable someone sitting or standing to see out of the window with ease.

Lining the opening with plasterboard
Section through window seen from the inside showing the lining on the side, top and bottom of the opening.

Cut the opening and fit the trimmers

HORIZONTAL TRIMMER
VERTICAL TRIMMER
CUT RAFTER
RAFTER
RAFTER

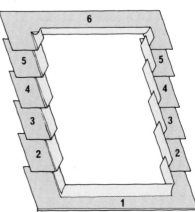

Flashing kit showing order of assembly

Using a pointing tray
A pointing tray makes the filling of mortar joints very easy. Place the flat lip of the tray just under a horizontal joint and scrape the mortar into place with a jointer. Turn the tray round and push mortar into vertical joints through the gap between the raised sides.

Continental-pattern trowels

● **Essential tools**
   Brick trowel
   Pointing trowel
   Plasterer's trowel
   Mortar board
   Hawk
   Spirit level
   Try square
   Plumb line

76

BUILDER'S TOOL KIT

Bricklayers, joiners and plasterers are all specialist builders, each requiring a set of specific tools, but the amateur is more like one of the self-employed builders who must be able to tackle several areas of building work, and so need a much wider range of tools than the specialist. The builder's tool kit suggested here is for renovating and improving the structure of a house and for erecting and restoring garden structures or paving. Electrical work, decorating and plumbing call for other sets of tools.

FLOATS AND TROWELS

For professional builders, floats and trowels have specific uses, but in home maintenance the small trowel for repointing brickwork is often found ideal for patching small areas of plaster, while the plasterer's trowel is as likely to be used for smoothing concrete.

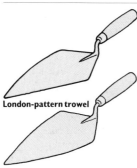

London-pattern trowel

Canadian-pattern trowel

Brick trowel
A brick trowel is for handling and placing mortar when laying bricks or concrete blocks. A professional might use one with a blade as long as 300mm (1ft), but such a trowel is too heavy and unwieldy for the amateur, so buy a good-quality brick trowel with a fairly short blade.
   The blade of a **London-pattern trowel** has one curved edge for cutting bricks, a skill that needs much practice to perfect. The blade's other edge is straight, for picking up mortar. This type of trowel is made in right- and left-handed versions, so be sure to buy the right one for you. A right-handed trowel has its curved edge on the right when you point it away from you.
   A Canadian-pattern trowel is symmetrical, so it's convenient when people with different left- and right-hand preferences want to share the one trowel.

Pointing trowel
The blade of a pointing trowel is no more than 75 to 100mm (3 to 4in) long, designed for repairing or shaping mortar joints between bricks.

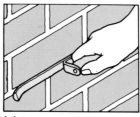

Jointer
A jointer is shaped for making 'V' or concave joints between bricks. The narrow blade is dragged along the mortar joint and the curved front end used for shaping the verticals.

Frenchman
A Frenchman is a specialized tool for cutting excess mortar away from brickwork jointing. You can make one by heating and bending an old table knife.

Wooden float
A wooden float is for applying and smoothing cement renderings and concrete to a fine attractive texture. The more expensive ones have detachable handles so that their wooden blades can be replaced when they wear, but the amateur is unlikely to use a float often enough to justify the extra cost.

Plasterer's trowel
A plasterer's trowel is a steel float for applying plaster and cement renderings to walls. It is also dampened and used for 'polishing', stroking the surface of the material when it has firmed up. Some builders prefer to apply rendering with a heavy trowel and finish it with a more flexible blade, but one has to be quite skilled to exploit such subtle differences.

BOARDS FOR CARRYING MORTAR OR PLASTER

Any convenient-sized sheet of 12 or 18mm (½ or ¾in) exterior-grade plywood can be used as a mixing board for plaster or mortar. A panel about 1m (3ft) square is ideal, and a smaller spotboard, about 600mm (2ft) square, is convenient for carrying the material to the actual work site. In either case screw some battens to the undersides of the boards to make them easier to lift and carry. Make a small lightweight hawk to carry pointing mortar or plaster by nailing a single batten underneath a plywood board so that you can plug a handle into it.

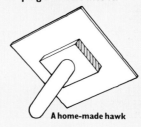

A home-made hawk

LEVELLING AND MEASURING TOOLS

You can make several specialized tools for measuring and levelling, but don't skimp on essentials like a good spirit level and a robust tape measure.

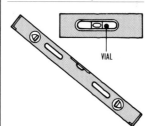

VIAL

Spirit level
A spirit level is a machine-made straightedge incorporating special glass tubes or vials that contain a liquid. In each vial an air bubble floats. When a bubble rests exactly between two lines marked on the glass the structure on which the level is held is known to be properly horizontal or vertical, depending on the vial's orientation. Buy a wooden or lightweight aluminium level 600 to 900mm (2 to 3ft) long. A well-made one is very strong, but treat it with care and always clean mortar or plaster from it before it sets.

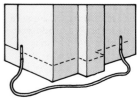

Water level
You can make a water level from a garden hose with short lengths of transparent plastic tube plugged into its ends. Fill the hose with water until it appears in both tubes. As water level is constant the levels in the tubes are always identical and so can be used for marking identical heights even over long distances and round obstacles and bends.

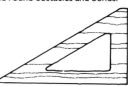

Builder's square
A large set square is useful when you set out brick or concrete-block corners. The best ones are stamped out of sheet metal, but you can make a serviceable one by cutting out a thick plywood right-angled triangle with a hypotenuse of about 750 mm (2ft 6in). Cut out the centre of the triangle to reduce the weight.

Checking a square
Accuracy is important, so check the square by placing it against a straight batten on the floor, drawing a line against the square to make a right angle with the batten, then turning the square to see if it forms the same angle from the other side.

Try square
Use a try square for marking out square cuts or joints on timber.

Making a plumb line
Any small but heavy weight hung on a length of fine string will make a suitable plumb line for judging the verticality of structures or surfaces.

Bricklayer's line

Use a bricklayer's line as a guide for laying bricks or blocks level. It is a length of nylon string stretched between two flat-bladed pins that are driven into vertical joints at the ends of a wall. There are also special line blocks that hook over the bricks at the ends of a course. As a makeshift you can stretch a string between two stakes driven into the ground outside the line of the wall.

Steel pins and line
Buy the special pins or make your own by hammering flats on 100mm (4in) nails.

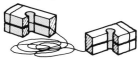

Line blocks
Blocks grip the brickwork corners; the line passes through their slots.

Plasterer's rule

A plasterer's rule is simply a straight wood batten used for scraping plaster and rendering undercoats level.

Straightedge

Any length of straight, fairly stout timber can be used to tell whether a surface is flat or, used with a spirit level, to test whether two points are at the same height.

Gauge stick

For gauging the height of brick courses, calibrate a softwood batten by making saw cuts across it at 75mm (3in) intervals – the thickness of a brick plus its mortar joint.

Tape measure

An ordinary retractable steel tape measure is adequate for most purposes but if you need to mark out or measure a large plot hire a wind-up tape up to 30m (100ft) in length.

Marking gauge

This tool has a sharp steel point for scoring a line on timber parallel to its edge. Its adjustable stock acts as a fence and keeps the point a constant distance from the edge.

HAMMERS

Very few hammers are needed on a building site.

Claw hammer
Choose a strong claw hammer for building wooden stud partitions, nailing floorboards, making door and window frames and putting up garden fencing.

Club hammer
A heavy club hammer is used for driving cold chisels and for various demolition jobs. It is also useful for driving large masonry nails into walls.

Sledgehammer
Hire a big sledgehammer if you have to break up hardcore or paving. It's also the best tool for driving stakes or fence posts into the ground, though you can make do with a club hammer if the ground is not too hard.

Mallet
A carpenter's wooden mallet is the proper tool for driving wood chisels, but you can use a hammer if the chisels have impact-resistant plastic handles.

SAWS

Every builder needs a range of handsaws, but consider hiring a power saw when you have to cut a lot of heavy structural timbers, and especially if you plan to rip floorboards down to width, a very tiring job when done by hand.

There are special power saws for cutting metal, and even for sawing through masonry.

Panel saw
All kinds of man-made building boards are used in house construction, so buy a good panel saw – useful also for cutting large structural timbers to the required lengths.

Tenon saw

A good saw for accurately cutting wall studs, floorboards, panelling and joints. The metal stiffening along the top of the blade keeps it rigid and less likely to wander off line.

Padsaw
Also called a keyhole saw, this small saw has a narrow tapered blade for cutting holes in timber.

Coping saw
A coping saw has a frame that holds a fairly coarse but very narrow blade under tension for cutting curves in wood.

Floorboard saw
If you prise a floorboard above its neighbours you can cut across it with an ordinary tenon saw, but a floorboard saw's curved cutting edge makes it easier to avoid damaging the boards on either side.

Hacksaw
The hardened-steel blades of a hacksaw have fine teeth for cutting metal. Use one to cut steel concrete-reinforcing rods or small pieces of sheet metal.

Sheet saw
A hacksaw's frame prevents its use for cutting large sheets of metal. For that job bolt a hacksaw blade to the edge of the flat blade of a sheet saw, which will also cut corrugated plastic sheeting and roofing slates.

Universal saw
A universal or general-purpose saw is designed to cut wood, metal, plastics and building boards. Its short frameless blade has a low-friction coating and is stiff enough to make straight cuts without wandering. The handle can be set at various angles. The saw is particularly useful for cutting secondhand timber, which may contain nails or screws that would blunt an ordinary woodsaw.

POWER SAWS

An electric **circular saw** will accurately rip timber or man-made boards down to size. As well as doing away with the effort of hand-sawing large timbers a sharp power saw produces such a clean cut that there is often no need for planing afterwards.

A **power jigsaw** will cut curves in timber and boards but is also useful for cutting holes in fixed wall panels and sawing through floorboards so as to lift them.

A **reciprocating saw** is a two-handed power saw with a long pointed blade, powerful enough to cut heavy timber sections and even through a complete stud partition, panels and all.

Masonry saw
A **power jigsaw** will cut wood handsaw but its tungsten-carbide teeth will cut brick, concrete blocks and stone.

DRILLS

A **reciprocating saw** is a *invaluable to a builder, but a hand brace is useful when you have to bore holes outdoors or in lofts and cellars that lack convenient electric sockets.*

Power drill
Buy a power drill, a range of twist drills and some spade or power-bore bits for drilling timber, and make sure that the tool has a percussion or hammer action for drilling masonry. For masonry you need special drill bits tipped with tungsten carbide. The smaller ones are matched to the size of standard wall plugs, though there are much larger ones with reduced shanks that can be used in a standard power-drill chuck. The larger bits are expensive, so hire them when you need them. Percussion bits are even tougher than masonry bits, with shatter-proof tips.

Brace and bit
A brace and bit is the ideal hand tool for drilling large holes in timber, and when fitted with a screwdriver bit it gives good leverage for driving or extracting large woodscrews.

Drilling masonry for wall plugs
Set the drill for low speed and hammer action, and wrap tape round the bit to mark the depth to be drilled. Allow for slightly more depth than the length of the plug as dust will pack down into the hole when you insert it. Drill the hole in stages, partly withdrawing the bit at times to clear the debris.

Protect floor coverings and paintwork from falling dust by taping a paper bag under the position of the hole before you start drilling.

● **Essential tools**
Straightedge
Tape measure
Claw hammer
Club hammer
Panel saw
Tenon saw
Hacksaw
Padsaw
Power drill
Masonry bits
Brace and bits

GLOSSARY OF TERMS

Architrave
The moulding around a door or window.

Bolster
A wide-bladed cold chisel for cutting bricks and concrete blocks. It is also useful for levering up floorboards.

Casing
The timber lining of a door opening.

Cavity wall
A wall of two separate masonry skins with an air-space between them.

Chase
A groove cut in masonry or plaster to accept pipework or an electrical cable. *or* To cut such grooves.

Cold chisel
A solid-metal octagonal-section chisel used to cut a chase in brickwork and plaster.

Cornice
The continuous horizontal moulding between walls and ceiling.

Coving
A pre-fabricated moulding used to make a cornice.

Dado
The lower part of an interior wall – usually defined with a moulded rail. *or* In the USA – a housing.

Damp-proof course
A layer of impervious material which prevents moisture rising from the ground into the walls of a building.

Damp-proof membrane
A layer of impervious material which prevents moisture rising through a concrete floor.

Dovetail nailing
A jointing technique using two nails driven at opposing angles to fix one piece of wood to the end grain of another.

DPC
See damp-proof course.
DPM
See damp-proof membrane.

Efflorescence
A white powdery deposit caused by soluble salts migrating to the surface of a wall or ceiling.

End grain
The surface of wood exposed after cutting across the fibres.

Flashing
A weatherproof junction between a roof and a wall or chimney, or between one roof and another.

Footing
A narrow concrete foundation for a wall.

Furring battens
See furring strips.
Furring strips
Parallel strips of wood fixed to a wall or ceiling to provide a framework for attaching panels.

Grounds
Strips of wood fixed to a wall to provide nail-fixing points for skirting boards and door casings. See also pallets.

Head plate
The top horizontal member of a stud partition.
Heave
An upward swelling of the ground caused by excess moisture.
Horns
Extended door or window stiles designed to protect the corners from damage while in storage.

Jamb
The vertical side member of a door or window frame.
Joist
A horizontal wooden or metal beam used to support a structure like a floor, ceiling or wall.

Key
To abrade or incise a surface to provide a better grip when gluing something to it.

Lath and plaster
A method of finishing a timber-framed wall or ceiling. Narrow strips of wood are nailed to the studs or joists to provide a supporting framework for plaster.
Lintel
A horizontal beam used to support the wall over a door or window opening.

Mastic
A non-setting compound used to seal joints.
Mullion
A vertical dividing member of a window frame.
Muntin
A central vertical member of a panel door.

Needle
A stout wooden beam used with props to support the section of a wall above an opening prior to the installation of an RSJ or lintel.
Nogging
A short horizontal wooden member between studs.
Nominal sizes
The standard sizes of sawn timber. Even planed timber is specified by nominal sizes because planed dimensions are not uniform.

Pallet
A wooden plug built into masonry to provide a fixing point for a door casing.
Party wall
The wall between two houses and over which each of the adjoining owners has equal rights.
Pinch rod
A wooden batten used to gauge the width of a door casing.

Reveal
The vertical side of an opening in a wall.
Rolled steel joist
A steel beam usually with a cross section in the form of a letter I.
RSJ
See rolled steel joist.

Sash
The openable part of a window.
Scratchcoat
The bottom layer of cement render.
Screed
A thin layer of mortar applied to give a smooth surface to concrete etc. *or* A shortened version of screed batten.
Screed batten
A thin strip of wood fixed to a surface to act as a guide to the thickness of an application of plaster or render.
Scribe
To copy the profile of a surface on the edge of sheet material which is to be butted against it. *or* To mark a line with a pointed tool.

Sill
The lowest horizontal member of a stud partition. *or* The lowest horizontal member of a door or window frame.
Sleeper wall
A low masonry wall used as an intermediate support for ground-floor joists.
Sole plate
Another term for a stud partition sill. *or* A wooden member used as a base to level a timber-framed loadbearing wall.
Staff bead
The innermost strip of timber holding a sliding sash in a window frame.
Stile
A vertical side member of a door or window sash.
Stretcher bond
The simplest form of brick bonding where the vertical joints are staggered by 50 per cent.
Stud partition
An interior timber-framed dividing wall.
Studs
The vertical members of a timber-framed wall.
Subsidence
A sinking of the ground caused by the shrinkage of excessively dry soil.

Transom
A horizontal dividing member of a window frame.

Vapour barrier
A layer of impervious material which prevents the passage of moisture-laden air.
Vapour check
See vapour barrier.

Wall flanges
Small metal flanges that clip onto each side of an electrical mounting box. The flanges fit behind a plasterboard wall lining, gripping it between them and the socket or switch faceplate.
Wall plate
A horizontal timber member placed along the top of a wall to support joists and to spread their load.